JUST
TEACH!
in FE

Sara Miller McCune founded SAGE Publishing in 1965 to support the dissemination of usable knowledge and educate a global community. SAGE publishes more than 1000 journals and over 800 new books each year, spanning a wide range of subject areas. Our growing selection of library products includes archives, data, case studies and video. SAGE remains majority owned by our founder and after her lifetime will become owned by a charitable trust that secures the company's continued independence.

Los Angeles | London | New Delhi | Singapore | Washington DC | Melbourne

JUST TEACH! in FE

A PEOPLE-CENTERED APPROACH

JIM CRAWLEY

Learning Matters
An imprint of SAGE Publications Ltd
1 Oliver's Yard
55 City Road
London EC1Y 1SP

SAGE Publications Inc.
2455 Teller Road
Thousand Oaks, California 91320

SAGE Publications India Pvt Ltd
B 1/I 1 Mohan Cooperative Industrial Area
Mathura Road
New Delhi 110 044

SAGE Publications Asia-Pacific Pte Ltd
3 Church Street
#10-04 Samsung Hub
Singapore 049483

Editor: Amy Thornton
Copy Editor: Fabienne Gray
Proof reader: Brian McDowell
Production Controller: Chris Marke
Project Management: Deer Park Productions
Marketing Manager: Lorna Patkai
Cover design: Wendy Scott
Typeset by: C&M Digitals (P) Ltd, Chennai, India
Printed and bound in the UK

First published in 2018 by Learning Matters Ltd

© Jim Crawley

Library of Congress Control Number: 2017957601

British Library Cataloguing in Publication Data

A catalogue record for this book is available from the British Library.

ISBN 978-1-5264-2475-4 (pbk)
ISBN 978-1-5264-2474-7

At SAGE we take sustainability seriously. Most of our products are printed in the UK using FSC papers and boards. When we print overseas we ensure sustainable papers are used as measured by the PREPS grading system. We undertake an annual audit to monitor our sustainability.

Dedication

To my eternally patient, beautiful and totally people-centred
Jan who makes every day worthwhile.

Contents

About the author

Jim Crawley has worked for 40 years in and with the Further Education sector, in teacher education, adult and community learning, education studies, professional development and basic skills. He has taught social and life skills, basic skills, on access to HE courses, and was an adult education organiser in the early 1980s. He even taught Computer Science O-Level for a part of one academic year (not well). Jim is still teaching new undergraduates about 'education for change' in Education Studies.

Jim has researched learning technology, teaching and learning and, in particular, teacher education, and he gained his PhD in 2014 after carrying out research into the professional situation of teacher educators in the FE sector. He has been involved in many small research projects with teachers, organisations and funders from FE and Higher Education.

For twelve years Jim co-ordinated the Bath Spa University Post Compulsory teacher education programme, which gained two consecutive outstanding grades in OfSTED Initial Teacher Education (ITE) inspections, and he is currently a part time Education Studies lecturer and a Teaching Fellow at Bath Spa University. Jim is the author of a wide range of articles, papers, reports and conference contributions on topics including Teacher Education, Learning Technology, and Adult and Community Education. He was the chair of the Post-16 Committee of the Universities' Council for the Education of Teachers (UCET) from 2012-15, and is currently also convenor of a national research network for FE teacher educators, called Teacher Education in Lifelong Learning (TELL).

Acknowledgements

Thanks to all the students I have taught over the years as they all made a difference to my teaching.

Thanks also to all the other teachers I have worked with. They knew nothing about it at the time, but they have provided much of what features in this book!

Thanks also to Amy Thornton. The final version of this book reads and looks much better because of her efforts as my editor.

Glossary

Apprenticeships   A means of combining practical training on the job with study in order to gain skills and knowledge in a specific job.

Assertiveness   Being able to state your needs and opinions with confidence and coherence in a range of situations.

Autonomy   The capacity to make decisions and take action based on one's individual judgement.

Continuing Professional Development (CPD)   The ongoing learning opportunities which help professionals to remain up to date and to improve their skills, knowledge and understanding.

Digital technology   Computer-based products and solutions.

Flipped learning   A pedagogical approach where students access online content individually at home before the teaching session, while in-class time is devoted to interactive exercises, projects, or discussions using and applying that content. This is termed 'flipping' the traditional teaching approach.

Ground rules   A set of rules for a group to work within, which are generated by the group themselves.

Initial Teacher Education   The training and support which is provided for teachers by other teachers to help them develop as education professionals and teaching practitioners, and provide them with an initial teaching qualification.

Lifelong learning   Learning for all which takes place throughout the lives of every member of the community.

Ofsted   Ofsted is a government, non-ministerial organisation. The Office for Standards in Education, Children's Services and Skills inspects and regulates services that care for children and young people, and services providing education and skills for learners of all ages.

Pedagogy   The practices and processes by which teaching is brought to life.

Performance indicators   A means of measuring performance against a set of pre-determined targets.

Social justice   The way in which equality and human rights are present in the everyday lives of all people at every level of society.

Social capital   The connections between individuals in communities which form networks for joint social action and from which greater trust in that community arises.

Social mobility   The ability of individuals, families or groups to move up or down the social ladder in a society, such as moving from working class to middle class.

Social network   A dedicated website or other application which enables users to communicate with each other by posting information, comments, messages, images, etc. Examples include Facebook and Twitter.

Sustainable Development   Development that meets the needs of the present, without compromising the ability of future generations to meet their own needs.

Teaching career   The ways in which a teaching professional's work develops and changes for them over an extended period of time, and the effect that has on them.

Teaching methods   The tools which are used in teaching sessions to manage and facilitate student learning. These can include practicals, demonstrations, lectures, discussion, games etc.

Teaching professional   A teacher working within a set of agreed values, practices, capabilities and philosophies which define and develop how they work as a practitioner.

Teaching resources   The items needed when teaching to enable the methods to succeed. These can include computers, raw materials, presentations, handouts, learning programmes etc.

Virtual Learning Environment (VLE)   An online system that allows teachers to share educational materials with their students via the web. Examples include Moodle and Blackboard.

Introduction

FE is different

Working in the English Further Education (FE) sector is different from working in any other part of the education sector. You will encounter a diversity of individuals as students, so you could be teaching 14 year olds and adults over 65 years in the same week (although probably not in the same session). The breadth and depth of their experience, the range of capabilities they possess and their learning needs can at times be bewildering. On other occasions however this diversity is genuinely inspiring.

The range and choice of subjects offered by FE providers, from FE colleges to adult education centres, and from military training schools to prison education is also much wider than that available at secondary school or university. There are also many types of courses or learning programmes. These can include full time courses over a number of years, part-time day or evening classes (although not as many as there were) and specially designed work-based training programmes. Some of the learning opportunities are online and a number use blended learning (a mix of face-to-face and online learning). There is no other part of UK education with more range and depth.

Overall, the FE sector offers local communities a rich tapestry of subjects, courses, services, opportunities and support. Because of these factors, a teacher in FE can also encounter more variety and diversity in what they teach, and who, when and where they teach it, than in other parts of the education sector. Embracing this natural variety and diversity is essential for you to both understand how FE works, and to recognise what a valuable job the FE sector does for society.

FE is challenging

There are also some well-documented challenges related to being a teacher in FE. The sector has a volatile nature which will surely be part of your working context as soon as you begin your career as a teaching professional, and there is every chance, based on the history of the sector over at least the last 25 years, that it will continue to be volatile for the foreseeable future. Teaching in FE at the time of writing takes place in an underfunded and undervalued environment, with ongoing austerity and perpetual change. This is not an easy combination to work with. Add this to the diversity, breadth and range which has just been discussed and you can end up with a long line of issues to manage before you get anywhere near a classroom, workshop or other teaching space.

Duckworth and Smith (2017: 2) point out a 'harsh reality' that 'central government policy interventions and cuts to public funding have resulted in the closure of courses, the loss of over a million adult learners, 15,000 experienced teachers and a similar number of support staff since 2009.' Unsurprisingly, this produces a teaching context which can be very difficult to understand and settle into, especially at the start of a teacher's career.

Many possibilities

Don't let this put you off. The change and volatility provides many possibilities for learning and development and the more fluid working situation in FE can give you more freedom in your teaching than you may come by in the more regulated school curriculum. There are many personal and professional challenges which you can learn to not just overcome, but to turn into positive opportunities for your students and your own development as a teacher. You will need resilience and a determination not to let the context distract you too much from the work you do, but this resilience and the approaches argued for in this book will help you teach in a more humane way, and help your students transform their lives.

What is the purpose of this book?

The book aims to be a straightforward, helpful, engaging and reliable companion on your professional journey which will be both immediately useful and a continuous source of advice and support for years to come. It is offered in a people-centred spirit of resistance to unfairness and inequality and promotes at its heart an unshakeable belief in the power of education, especially in FE, to transform people's lives. It is not designed as a teacher education course text book, but it naturally addresses many key topics contained in teacher education courses, so will be helpful in supporting study on teacher education programmes and for continuing professional development. The content is referenced on an ongoing basis to leading edge education research and thinking to support its key ideas.

Some books aimed at new or trainee teachers (and often those aimed at experienced teachers too) pay a great deal of attention to what teachers are expected to teach and how they are expected to do it. That is perfectly reasonable given the concentration on external expectations in the shape of national teaching standards; inspections by the Office for Standards in Education (Ofsted); government monitored outcomes for recruitment, retention and achievement; and impact measures about almost every aspect of teaching, learning, management and organisation. This emphasis does however tend to consign some of the key principles and practices at the heart of teaching into components in a tool box, to be taken out and used when needed.

More than a toolkit

Although that can be helpful at times, teaching is about so much more than tools in a toolbox. The toolbox approach places a straitjacket on the process of understanding what teaching and learning are about, and leads to the impression that there are solutions and strategies which can be applied like ingredients in a recipe, and which will lead to the perfect teaching cake every time. The way people learn is just not that predictable, and qualities such as motivation, self-confidence and creativity play a significant part in helping human beings to learn (or of course in preventing them from learning). How these qualities may develop though learning is very difficult, if not impossible to accurately capture in detail, or to measure, and they can therefore be relegated to second order importance in a teacher education curriculum, or in Continuing Professional Development (CPD) for teachers, if they are even included. This book places them at its heart.

The approach and structure of the book

I have consciously used ideas, thinking and research from any source which I have considered to be useful and relevant, and some of the ideas and activities are from what I would describe as 'vintage teaching sources' which I have really enjoyed rediscovering while writing this book. Contemporary thinking, activities and ideas are also utilised, including very recent research and development and I have often stepped outside the FE sector to find relevant research, as the other sectors of education tend to have a wider range of attention paid to them by researchers. I have provided opportunities for the reader to come at some of the topics, techniques, theories and strategies offered from more than one perspective so that different readers can make use of what makes most sense to them.

The overall approach and structure aims to demystify the early stages of teaching for new teachers, and help them ride out the inevitable waves of change across at least the start of their teaching careers. You will be asked to consider a number of well-known (and some not so well-known) ideas about education and society and to reflect on how these ideas may (or may not) fit with your own ideas, experiences, values and world view. I hope that the process of reflection and action involved will provoke a strong response in favour of the ideas within.

Chapter format

Each chapter begins with a list of 'key learning points' which are the principal themes of that chapter, and the chapter moves through those key learning points in turn. At the end of each chapter a 'this chapter' summary is included to reinforce the messages from that chapter. There are also 'Notes for further reading', featuring a small selection of the sources used in each chapter, which I would especially recommend. The final element of each chapter is a list of the Professional Standards for Teachers and Trainers (Education and Training Foundation, 2014) which have been addressed by the chapter. The complete list of all references used in the book is at the end of all the chapters.

Each chapter contains activities, practical examples from the field of teaching and learning, and regular opportunities to think about and apply pedagogy, or the study of the theory and practice of teaching. These are included in the following ways.

Reflective learning exercises

'Reflective learning exercises' are intended to provide points of reflection to facilitate deeper learning, and these are mainly represented by 'acts of connection'. These are activities for your own use in your own teaching, with other colleagues in your organisation or for your students to use. The reflective learning features link in with the key learning points of the chapter.

Spotlight on pedagogy

A 'spotlight on pedagogy', such as much of the content in the section on learning theory, highlights the thinking behind some of the practices of teaching featured in this book, but without the inclusion of an accompanying activity.

These spotlights and the reflective learning exercises are all examples of 'people-centred teaching' and will be linked together to help you to develop and grow your practice as a teacher in ways which will improve the learning of your students.

The chapters

The book has seven chapters, organised in three parts. Part 1 is 'Introducing people centred teaching and learning'; part 2 is 'Just teach'; and part 3 is 'Just keep teaching'.

'Chapter 1 – Introducing people-centred teaching for connected professionals' is the first of two in part 1 and introduces the key ideas, approaches and concepts of the book. A definition of the FE sector and its historical context is provided, and the book's underpinning philosophy of 'people-centred teaching' is explained. 'Acts of connection' or small, connected steps in teaching, learning and professional development are then introduced to suggest how it is possible to build and make connections along the journey to becoming a more expert teacher, or a 'connected professional'. There is also an introduction to some of the personal characteristics and qualities with which people-centred teaching engages.

Chapter 2 – What did learning theories ever do for me? This is the second chapter of part 1, and begins with a proposed set of professional values for FE. The rest of the chapter presents a range of learning theories, explains their key points and where the ideas came from, their relevance to people-centred teaching and some of the critiques of each theory.

Chapters 3 to 6 are part 2 and in turn they introduce, build and develop the different aspects, ideas, practices and processes of people-centred teaching. Each of these four chapters addresses one 'just teach' key theme and provides examples, reflective incidents and activities for the reader to use to support their own exploration of their teaching. The content of each chapter is linked to the four connections of the 'connected professional' as they occur.

'Chapter 3 – Building and keeping trust' provides a series of teaching strategies, activities and techniques for building trust in your own teaching and in your work with other teachers. Evidence about how building trust works to enhance student confidence, motivation and creativity, and the impact this can have on student achievement is considered. The importance of teacher collaboration and 'relational leadership' is discussed, the positive value of 'golden moments' in teaching and learning emphasised, and how to positively manage 'troubled times' is considered.

'Chapter 4 – Be organised' takes the reader through 'getting your head organised'; 'getting your heart organised'; 'getting your teaching organised'; 'helping your students get organised'; and finally 'starting to get your career organised'. These themes are all linked to how you can develop your teaching and career in a range of practical ways by being organised.

'Chapter 5 – Be connected' uses the metaphor of the 'digital swamp' to highlight some of the challenges, issues and mistakes which education has already made, and continues to make when using digital technologies. Research evidence about what can and does work is used to help you to escape from the digital swamp, and the use of 'network learning' is recommended as one way of doing so. How to make use of digital technologies in work with the broader community and a 'technology for all manifesto' in the shape of a plea to 'maketechhuman' complete this chapter.

'Chapter 6 – Come together and stand together' highlights how education is in the global spotlight, and how inequality in our own country is still present and can be combated in FE. The chapter then considers the use of 'critical reflection' to help teachers 'mix and match' their teaching choices, strategies and approaches to best suit the situation they are working in and the needs of their students. Practitioner research is recommended to assist FE teachers 'stand together to stand out' and to help them extend the transformative benefits of people-centred teaching in FE to all.

'Chapter 7 – Just keep teaching – teaching and learning careers' concludes the book by introducing a 'growth mindset' and how this can be used to develop teacher and student resilience. Practical advice about managing different pressures including those arising from inspections then follows. Promoting positive 'learning careers' with your students and positive 'teaching careers' for all teachers is introduced before a reminder of the key ideas and thinking about the practice of people-centred teaching which have been contained in chapters 1 to 6.

The book closes with an appeal to all teachers to sign up to people-centred teaching.

Overall, the book blends long-established and more recent principles of teaching and learning and encourages the reader to take the ideas and examples, and apply them in their own teaching situation to become people-centred teachers.

Over more than 40 years of working in and with the FE sector, I've seen, worked with, tried and avoided many different approaches and ideas which are supposed to lead to 'outstanding learner achievement '. Some of them even did. They come and go depending on who oversees your college, training department, charity or organisation, which party or parties are in government and which government minister is in charge. They are often under tested and poorly researched. They are sometimes quite surreal in their conception, and have clearly been devised by people who do not regularly teach, or even get very near to a teaching location! We are often either strongly encouraged, or even required to use them in our efforts to get a good Ofsted result, or better examination results, student retention statistics and better recruitment as part of our everyday professional life.

People-centred teaching functions at a much more simple and natural level than that. A positive, human connection between you and your students is crucial and contributing to the same positive connection between them and their peers is equally important. When I started teaching, working with lively, disengaged and unemployed teenagers, looking for ways to make connections with them was a natural way to get started. Working with this idea, which at that stage was just an idea and a strong feeling, helped me to promote engagement, start confidence building and encourage the young people involved to work towards the possibilities of small positive achievements, rather than reinforcing their feelings of disadvantage and demotivation. There was nothing to stop me reflecting on my own responses, reactions and ideas, and trying them out in my teaching (apart from the fact that the teenagers concerned would make it clear to me if they didn't think what I was suggesting they do was worth a try!) My capability to teach developed steadily, and my confidence that it was working also seemed to be validated by the much more positive results being achieved by my students. No one produced any performance indicators at the time, as we built them ourselves together, but we all knew what was working, why and how.

Over a long period of time, the FE sector has drifted away from encouraging and respecting teacher autonomy and professionalism, and moved into a 'must do' approach where those not teaching almost always exert the main influence on what those who are teaching do. There is no logic in this way of working. In discussions with teachers you can quickly appreciate that much great teaching, great learning and indeed great contributions to outstanding achievement does exist everywhere in the sector. What is often also mentioned however is that this is despite what their organisation or government does to support them, rather than because of it.

Just Teach provides an alternative for Further Education to over-controlled, outcomes-driven and ever-changing teaching and that is 'people-centred teaching' by 'connected professionals'. This reminds us that learning is an essential part of human engagement in building a better future for us all, not a dehumanised set of performance indicators.

What we are good at in FE is 'just teaching', so please let us 'just teach'.

Part 1

Introducing people centred teaching and learning

Chapter 1

Introducing people-centred teaching for connected professionals

 Key learning points in this chapter

The context and nature of the FE sector

Explaining 'people-centred teaching' and 'acts of connection'

Working towards becoming a 'connected professional'

We are all human – which characteristics are addressed by people-centred teaching?

The context and nature of the FE sector

Since the eighteenth century 'Further Education' has existed in the UK in a form which has some resemblance to that taking place today. The early work took the form of literary and philosophical societies, the first of which was founded in Manchester in 1781. The Anderson Institute, founded in 1796, was 'the first in the world to provide evening classes in science and the first to admit women on the same terms as men' (Walker, 2012: 32). Mechanics Institutes were established in 1823 to provide training in areas that were relevant to industry. Walker (2012: 32) argues that Mechanics Institutes provided 'a firm foundation on which technical and vocational education was established by the beginning of the twentieth century and has continued to date'. Fisher and Simmons (2010: 7) chart a 'burst of activity that encouraged growth of technical and commercial post school education' during the twentieth century. The arrival of the 1944 Education Act placed a statutory responsibility on local authorities to 'provide adequate facilities' for what was for the first time named 'Further Education' (Butler Act, 1944). The pace of change accelerated from the 1960s, and more activity across a wider range of subjects and learners, the creation of more sub-sectors and regular changes of sector titles became part of the ongoing context within which teaching took place. By 2015, the somewhat surreal situation had been arrived at where, 'in the three decades up to the 2015 election there had been 61 Secretaries of State responsible for skills policy in Britain', and there had been '13 major acts of parliament'. As if that isn't enough, the responsibility for skills policy had changed government department or been shared 'on ten different occasions' (Orr, 2016: 19). The Lingfield report (DBIS, 2012) recommended the withdrawal of a requirement for teachers in FE to gain a teaching qualification, only 12 years after it was introduced. At the time of writing another major piece of education legislation, the 'Technical and Further Education Act, 2017' has been passed, and this institutes another range of significant changes for the sector. Overall, it is not an exaggeration to argue that FE stands at the centre of a change and policy vortex.

If you work in Primary Education, Secondary or Higher Education, most people outside the sector will have a reasonably clear idea of where that fits in the overall education sector. If you mention 'primary' or 'secondary' in a conversation, people's eyes show recognition. Even here though, it has become harder to pinpoint what exactly a primary school or secondary school is called. Within the overall terms 'primary' and 'secondary' there are now many different types of school, but they are still called 'primary' and 'secondary' education. Higher Education, although it takes place in places other than universities, also retains a consistent title in its various contexts and locations.

Naming the sector

Naming this sector, which we are calling Further Education in this book, is however a different matter. Other parts of the education sector do not seem to have such an identity crisis. In the last 20 years, FE has had several different titles including Post Compulsory Education and Training, Post Compulsory Education, Lifelong Learning, Learning and Skills, Further Education and Training and currently Further Education and Skills. These are only some of the more 'official' definitions (i.e. those favoured or created by governments). There have been many others suggested by writers, organisations and professional groupings, including 'Further, Adult and Vocational Education' (FAVE) to name just one. When you are in a conversation with someone who does not work in the FE sector, and you mention 'Further Education' or 'Post Compulsory Education' people's eyes become glazed, as they genuinely don't quite know what you are talking about. This is not a good starting position for the sector.

Defining FE

Despite the regularly changing name, and an underlying difficulty describing just which educational activities are included in FE, it is possible to define what the sector does, if not necessarily what it is called. The best way of defining 'Further Education' is by including its component parts. This does not necessarily give you a clear brand of education, but it does at least make clear what is involved. What follows is an inclusive definition, which I created in Crawley (2010) and which will be meaningful to readers, as they will be able to identify their own position in the sector from this definition. For this book, the Further Education sector includes teaching and learning activity in

---

further education colleges, adult and community learning and development centres, workplace learning organisations, 14–19 college provision, sixth form colleges, public services or armed forces training or offender learning, none of which is delivered by school teachers.

(Adapted from Crawley, 2010: 14)

The size and scale of FE

It is also important to remind ourselves that FE works with a very large number of people.

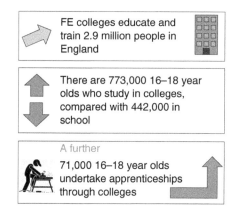

FE colleges educate and train 2.9 million people in England

There are 773,000 16–18 year olds who study in colleges, compared with 442,000 in school

A further

71,000 16–18 year olds undertake apprenticeships through colleges

Complex, varied and difficult to name it may be, but the FE sector still educates a very significant number of people each year.

Explaining 'people-centred teaching' and 'acts of connection'

Spotlight on pedagogy

People-centred teaching – Dewey and Freire

There is no shortage of leading thinkers, old and new, who believe that education is and should be centred on people. John Dewey (1859-1952) argued that learning is not just about outcomes or bodies of knowledge but that it is focused on the lifelong growth of the learner as a person with feelings, interests, needs and preoccupations. Dewey insisted that education is the heart of a democratic society, and that members of an educated society would be able to critically engage with each other through their experiences to create a better world. Dewey's vision was based more on reflecting on the ideas of others than empirical research, but his views remain extremely influential over 100 years later.

Paulo Freire (1973) reinforced this philosophy of education as offering many possibilities to improve the world, and emphasised how it can help people act together for change. His work helping oppressed minorities in South America to become literate contributed to the development of his vision of education as a liberating and empowering process. He argued that learning helps people to increase their understanding of their own situation and, as a result, their own confidence in their ability to do something about it. This growth in confidence and self-awareness can empower individuals and groups to become involved in action together, with the express intent of improving their life situation. These actions then contribute to reducing and ultimately removing the oppression people face and changing their world for the better.

Spotlight on pedagogy

Recent people-centred teaching approaches – Illeris and Jarvis

People-centred approaches to teaching and learning are not however a relic from the past and only found in the works of thinkers who are no longer with us. As the editor of a 2010 book on current educational thought by current educational thinkers, Knud Illeris, who is a professor of lifelong learning at the Danish University of Education (and is still very much alive), exemplifies how current thinking also embraces a people-centred approach to teaching and learning. Illeris firstly acknowledges how education has become 'a crucial parameter of competition in the present globalised market and knowledge society'. He then powerfully reminds us that education is much more than that, when he insists that it 'is, however, important to emphasise that the competitive functions of learning are merely a secondary, late-modern addition to the much more fundamental primary function of learning as one of the most basic abilities and manifestations of human life' (Illeris, 2010: 1). He further asserts that this 'far-reaching type of learning' can lead to 'changes in the organisation of the self' which can result in 'both profound and extensive transformative learning' (ibid: 14). In contrast to that greater purpose for education, he suggests that 'in schools, in education, at workplaces and in many other situations, very often people do not learn what they could learn or what they are supposed to learn' (ibid: 15).

Peter Jarvis, one of the best-known living figures in the field of adult learning, argues that 'fundamentally, it is the person who learns and it is the changed person who is the outcome of the learning'. The individual as a social being is also 'crucial to our understanding of learning' as is 'the fact that the person is both mind and body' (Jarvis, 2010: 25). Jarvis continues that individuals, as they change, 'cannot make this meaning alone; we are social human beings' and that 'as we change and others change as they learn, the social world is always changing' (Jarvis, 2010: 26).

Is our current education system people-centred?

As will become clear through the different sections of this book, the belief that learning is people-centred is strongly supported by a wide range of thinkers, many of whom have carried out extensive research which has led to this conclusion. When comparing this evidence with the existing education systems across the UK however, there is less evidence that it is as people-centred as we would hope for. There is a strong emphasis on learner outputs, learning outcomes and impact measures, an over-reliance on data and a growing culture of ongoing monitoring and inspection in all education, and particularly in FE. It appears that, for governments, education is too important to set it free. This emphasis on counting and measuring, albeit in the name of accountability and quality improvement, has created a situation which Biesta has called 'valuing what we measure' rather than 'measuring what we value' (2010: 13). I have spent 40 years as a teacher and I have seen control by organisations and governments over teachers grow to the point where education is moving along a path towards sterility and a lack of humanity. This is desperately unfair on students, and on those trying to teach them, and is not leading to a better, more equal society.

If we can work together to draw the human features back into the centre of how we organise education, we may just be able to rescue learning before it is too late. I strongly believe that using people-centred approaches in teaching and learning is a logical, evidence-based way of organising education. This is not the voice of opinion or merely my experience, but the evidence from research at many levels, as we shall see. It is not of course the only approach which can work, but the book argues in detail how it can succeed.

Spotlight on pedagogy

The process of education

As can be seen from the previous section, the concept of 'people-centred teaching' represents a vision of education as an ongoing process, drawing individuals, groups and communities together to support them in determining and achieving their own goals, destiny and purpose. This springs from a belief that individuals and groups are, as humans, naturally able to learn, work and live together and that education can provide opportunities to help that process to work at all levels.

Etienne Wenger explained this idea exceptionally well in 2010. The following extract is long, but it is included as I could not paraphrase it any better. Wenger begins by stating that education is

> largely based on the assumption that learning is an individual process, that it has a beginning and an end, that it is best separated from the rest of our activities, and that it is the result of teaching. Hence we arrange classrooms where students - free from the distractions of their participation in the outside world - can pay attention to a teacher or focus on exercises.

> To assess learning, we use tests with which students struggle in one-on-one combat, where knowledge must be demonstrated out of context, and where collaborating is considered cheating. As a result, much of our institutionalized teaching and training is perceived by would-be learners as irrelevant, and most of us come out of this treatment feeling that learning is boring and arduous, and that we are not really cut out for it.

> So what if we adopted a different perspective, one that placed learning in the context of our lived experience of participation in the world? What if we assumed that learning is as much a part of human nature as eating?'

> (Wenger, 2010: 209-210)

Wenger's proposed approach to make the most of learning is through participation. He argues that 'participation here refers not just to local events of engagement in certain activities with certain people, but to a more encompassing process of being active participants in the practices of social communities and constructing identities in relation to these communities' (2010: 210).

Reflective learning exercise

Acts of connection

Elkjaer also argues that learning is an interaction or transaction from which people learn and that 'it is possible to learn from experience, because experience can be used to create connections to the past and the future' (Elkjaer, 2010: 82). I am proposing in this book that participation in those

(Continued)

(Continued)

'events of engagement', and the creation of 'connections to the past and future', should be one of the most significant roles of a teacher, and that the vehicle for the construction and sharing of those experiences should be 'acts of connection'. Teaching should help to develop, organise, link together and facilitate experiences from which learners can participate in acts of connection. Throughout this book, activities, examples and ideas will be included as 'acts of connection' and as part of the inclusion of reflective learning exercises. You are asked to try them out and use them in your own teaching, and they are intended to be a diverse and helpful set of activities for all teachers and for their students. The first 'act of connection' follows.

Reflective learning exercise

Act of connection – positive and negative experiences of learning

Think back over your life and choose two learning experiences, one negative and one positive. Ask these questions about each learning experience in turn.

- What was the situation and what did you learn?
- Who or what caused that learning to be negative or positive?
- How did you feel about that learning experience then, and how do you feel about it now?
- How did that learning connect to other later experiences in your life or work?

The results of this activity can be very helpful in discussing learning from a personal perspective, but also in finding or establishing connections between your own or your students' previous experiences of learning, and how they approach their current learning. It is always surprising how powerful negative and positive experiences of learning are for participants, and the effect they have on people's lives, so take care when using this and activities like this, as bad memories and good memories can resurface.

The 'connected professional'

If we are starting as professionals on a shared journey towards people-centred teaching where we help our learners experience and learn from acts of connection, it is only reasonable to describe the teaching professional needed to fulfil this role. I'm arguing that this is a job for 'the connected professional'. The concept of a 'connected professional' (Crawley, 2015) draws on a variety of practitioners and thinkers on professionalism including Dzur (2008), Freire (1973), Fuller and Unwin (2003), Lave and Wenger (1991), Sachs (2000) and Schön (1983). I am arguing that this is the right model for FE teaching professionals in the twenty-first century. The key concept is that a connected professional will be able to help students make those connections which can lead to learning, and that they will also seek to work through connections with other teaching professionals and the community at large. They will create and use acts of connection to help their students learn in a people-centred way.

Spotlight on pedagogy

The four connections of the connected professional

The model of the Connected Professional contains four 'connections', which are:

1 *The Practical Connection* – The practical teaching skills, knowledge, understanding and application which are essential for all teachers to be able to carry out their role.

2 *The Democratic Connection* – The active involvement in action where practitioners work together democratically with other colleagues towards agreed goals.

3 *The Civic Connection* – Active participation in civic action with the wider community to support development with and for that community.

4 *The Networked Connection* – Seeking, undertaking and sustaining active engagement with other professionals and the wider community.

The first three connections can be 'switched on' by the fourth, the Networked Connection. This idea makes use of the notion of 'network learning'. Veugelers and O'Hair (2005) describe 'network learning' as a process which helps teaching professionals learn and teach together more effectively through the process of networking. Digital technology is important to facilitating that process, but the process is more important than the technology. This brief discussion of the connected professional is by way of an introduction. Ways of understanding and applying this concept further are spread throughout the book.

We are all human – which characteristics are addressed by people-centred teaching?

It may be difficult to remember this during a wearying and less-than-successful teaching session, when you are undergoing an observation of your teaching, or when an inspection takes place, but we are of course all people. Students, teachers, administrators, managers, inspectors, and even government ministers are all people. We are all at our best some of the time and at our worst some of the time and teachers need to remind themselves of that regularly. People are made up of many feelings, emotions, qualities and characteristics, and helping to blend those into confident students who achieve deep learning, their goals and a better life is not easy.

A number of the characteristics of people are however particularly relevant to teaching and learning, and they are empathy and trust; self-concept; motivation and aspiration; creativity and communication. I have paired some of these qualities and characteristics together because I believe they interact constructively with each other in a way that can start to help the connections we seek to make happen. These are not the only qualities and characteristics which are important, but together they provide a basis for people-centred teaching and they flow together to demonstrate the potential for making connections at every stage of teaching and learning. They are briefly introduced in this chapter and explored further in later chapters.

Empathy and trust

I'm starting with empathy and trust, because they are absolute essentials if you are ever going to help your students achieve a positive self-concept, maintain motivation, aspire to better lives, think and behave creatively, and communicate in a clear and meaningful way. An emphasis on empathy, which is a sensing or understanding by one person of the feelings and personal meanings of another, can be problematic. It is not always easy in all situations to have empathy with all students as a teacher. You are bound to feel more positively about some than others. Awakening and using your empathy for other human beings, however, can provide that starting point for meaningful learning. Brandes and Ginnis include these basic assumptions in their classic book on 'student centred learning', when they state that 'we can purposefully and yet with integrity adopt a stance of unconditional positive regard for the person, to which the person may, sooner or later, respond with trust' (Brandes and Ginnis, 1996: 5). They then draw on thinking from Carl Rogers (1961: 33) to add, 'if we can provide a certain relationship, the other person can discover within himself the capacity to use that relationship for growth, and change and personal development will occur'.

This readiness to show empathy leads to a process which Weare (2004: 4) argues builds up 'trust that is the bedrock of [learning] relationships.' If the learners can't trust the teacher, they won't take the risks or accept the challenges which lead to successful learning.

Self-concept

Empathy and trust can really make a difference when working as a teacher, and in the rest of our lives, and one of the most important characteristics in students which can be nurtured and maintained through an empathetic and trusting learning relationship is self-concept. Self-concept is the way each person sees themselves, and it is also possible for groups of people to have a group self-concept. Brandes and Ginnis (1996: 16) suggest that we should help students be co-creators of a learning process which will result in them seeing themselves 'differently as a result of the learning experience'. Our goal as teachers is to help our students to develop and maintain individual and group self-concepts that are more confident, self-directing and open to learning.

Motivation and aspiration

These two characteristics are paired because motivation and aspiration are closely linked in combining to form the self-concept of students. Motivation is the internal force which, at its simplest, relates to us meeting our individual needs. Aspiration is the hope that we will achieve something in our lives. Motivation and aspiration can either help or hinder learning, and they can also be strongly influenced by external forces, experiences and circumstances. Some of the students who are in FE have not always been motivated by their previous experiences of learning, and their life situations have resulted in a lack of aspirations. They can also be strongly resistant to change. A people-centred teacher takes the standpoint put forward by Brandes and Ginnis, that there 'is a natural motivation, not one created by carrot and stick. Motivation grows from within' (1996: 173). Aspiration is also especially important in developing and sustaining motivation because it is shaped early, and is 'modified by experience and the environment'. It can also decline as people mature, and 'this decline is particularly marked for those facing multiple barriers' (Gutman and Akerman, 2008: 5).

Creativity

'Creativity is the greatest gift of human intelligence. The more complex the world becomes, the more creative we need to be to meet its challenges. Yet many people wonder if they have any creative abilities at all.' This classic Ken Robinson quote (2011: xiii) opens one of his many writings about the need to ensure that creativity is cultivated 'in business, in education and in everyday life' (2011: xiv). Robinson argues that creativity is one of the most essential qualities needed in a constantly changing and complex world and that 'now, more than ever, we need to exercise the unique creative powers that make us humans in the first place' (2011: 17).

Communication

This seems like a less exciting and more mundane human quality or characteristic, but without a capacity to communicate, we are all unlikely to be able to work successfully with each other, and with the other qualities and characteristics listed here. This is another part of education which has a government-inspired identity crisis, as we never seem to know whether communication belongs in social and life skills (a golden oldie); life skills; core skills; key skills; functional skills; literacy; basic skills and of course more recently Language, Literacy and Numeracy (LLN) or English and Mathematics. The amount of time wasted in deciding on standards and specifications in this field adds up to several lifetimes, but we'll keep it simple in this book. What is understood by communication here is 'being able to get along with other people, to communicate clearly and with empathy for the listener' (Robinson, 2011: 175).

As has already been said, there are many ways to teach and learn, and there are many human qualities and characteristics involved. Teaching is certainly not easy and, currently, the FE sector has some difficult challenges for us all to undertake.

Reflective learning exercise

Act of connection – How people-centred is your teaching now?

Having identified empathy and trust, self-concept, motivation and aspiration, and creativity and communication as key human characteristics on which people-centred teaching focuses, take some time to rate yourself against how well you are able now to establish and develop these characteristics with and in your students:

Characteristics	Rating 1 to 5
	(1 is low, 5 is high)
Empathy and trust	
Positive self-concept	
Motivation and aspiration	
Creativity	
Communication	

The maximum score is 25, and I would never expect any teacher to reach and sustain that level, but you would want to be aiming for around 20 overall.

This chapter

This chapter has discussed the context and nature of the FE sector and provided a definition of what it actually does. The central concepts of 'people-centred teaching' have been introduced, and the first reflective learning exercises have been included as 'acts of connection', as have the first spotlights on pedagogy. What is involved in becoming a 'connected professional' and how that should fit within the teaching profession in FE has also been outlined. The chapter closes by identifying seven human characteristics which are addressed by people-centred teaching, and asks the reader to self-assess where they would consider themselves in that journey at this point in time.

Further reading notes

Brandes, D. and Ginnis, P. (1996) *A guide to student-centred learning*. Leicester: Nelson Thornes.

You should be able to access at least some of this resource on Google books. This classic teaching book is perhaps a bit dated now in some ways, but contains many good ideas and activities which should encourage any teacher to be more student-centred. It's written in a clear, straightforward style and contains many activities to make your teaching more student-centred.

Illeris, K. (ed.) (2010) *Contemporary theories of learning*. London: Routledge.

This book gives you a good selection of relatively brief essays about learning by 16 of the best known people in the field. It is not all straightforward reading, but you can choose the ones which make most sense to you. The book will genuinely help any teacher deepen their understanding of learning and some of the best current research and thinking in the field.

www.infed.org or 'infed' (used to be called the 'informal education' website)

This website describes itself as follows:

> 'we specialize in the theory and practice of informal education, social pedagogy, lifelong learning, social action, and community learning and development.'

The website contains a really good range of details of thinkers, ideas and concepts, and I would consider it a 'must visit', free resource for anyone interested in education.

National Standards which are addressed by this chapter are:

1. Reflect on what works best in your teaching and learning to meet the diverse needs of learners.

2. Evaluate and challenge your practice, values and beliefs.

3. Inspire, motivate and raise aspirations of learners through your enthusiasm and knowledge.

4. Be creative and innovative in selecting and adapting strategies to help learners to learn.

5. Value and promote social and cultural diversity, equality of opportunity and inclusion.

6. Build positive and collaborative relationships with colleagues and learners.

8. Maintain and update your knowledge of educational research to develop evidence-based practice.

11. Manage and promote positive learner behaviour.

13. Motivate and inspire learners to promote achievement and develop their skills to enable progression.

15. Promote the benefits of technology and support learners in its use.

16. Address the mathematics and English needs of learners and work creatively to overcome individual barriers to learning.

17. Enable learners to share responsibility for their own learning and assessment, setting goals that stretch and challenge.

As this is an introductory chapter, almost all national standards are addressed at least to some degree.

Chapter 2

What did learning theories ever do for me?

 Key learning points in this chapter

Professional values for our time.

What are learning theories and why do we need them?

Learning theories to enrich learning and teaching

Learning as a pathway to freedom

Professional values for our time

Before we start to engage in more detail with the principles and practices associated with people-centred teaching, it is time to introduce the professional values which should be the bedrock for people-centred teaching in Further Education. The philosophies and ideas explored in Chapter 1 are all underpinned by this set of values, as is the vision of teaching, learning and society that they represent.

 Spotlight on pedagogy

FE transforms lives

The work that FE undertakes is extremely important. Duckworth and Smith (2017: 3) argue that the 'FE sector is vital in transforming lives and communities in 21st century Britain' and that FE:

(Continued)

(Continued)

- provides an opportunity for the integration of marginalised and often silenced communities

- offers a stream of social capital which enriches learners' personal lives, enabling the formation of supportive bonds with other learners

- brings about transformation in the selfhood and social identities of learners with few or no qualifications, reintegrating them as active survivors with renewed hope and determination in our country's rapidly changing economy

- is a powerful vehicle to drive forward social justice.

(Duckworth and Smith, 2017: 8)

In order to contribute fully to the sector's transformative nature, teaching professionals need to align themselves with a set of values which are relevant and appropriate for that broader community-facing focus. These values will also help to establish a genuinely positive concept of what constitutes a teaching professional in the sector. FE teachers need a positive professional self-concept as much as our students need their own individual or group positive self-concept. The professional values asserted here are challenging, but should be expected of teaching professionals in FE. They have been devised from sector-based research, among others, from Crawley (2015) and Duckworth (2016).

 Spotlight on pedagogy

Professional values for people-centred teachers

The people-centred professional values of teachers in FE should be to:

- Conduct their profession with honesty, integrity and transparency within the public domain.

- Accept responsibility for a social purpose within their specialism and a broader purpose in the wider community beyond that.

- Embrace the responsibility to work with other professionals and the wider community.

- Support students through their commitment, humanity, organisation and professional expertise.

- Find ways of improving teaching and learning.

- Care for each other as a fundamental prerequisite for mental and emotional well-being.

- Demonstrate autonomy within their professional practice.

- Participate in decisions affecting their professional lives and environments.

- Subject their work to public accountability.

- Selflessly commit to updating their expertise and continuous development of their field.

What are learning theories and why do we need them?

There is a well-known and well-used website called www.learning-theories.com (which I would thoroughly recommend visiting if you haven't already done so). There are almost 70 theories listed and explained on this website, so as you can see, there is no shortage of learning theories. Fenwick and Tennant (2004) argue that there is no single learning theory which is more powerful or meaningful than all the others, because learning occurs in all aspects of life, not in a laboratory or control group. The context of a person's life exerts a very strong influence over their experiences and life situation, and this of course influences how they are engaged, or not engaged, in learning.

Firstly, here is a simple definition of what a learning theory is.

A learning theory is a group of ideas which attempt to explain what happens when people learn.

 *Spotlight on pedagogy*

Seven factors underpinning successful learning?

By way of introduction to the thinkers and theorists to follow, here is a good example of how a teacher can find out for themselves what helps people to learn. Phil Race is a very experienced and skilled teacher who runs courses and seminars across many locations around the world, and he wished to understand more clearly what the participants he worked with felt helped them to learn. Over a 30-year period, Phil has regularly asked his participants, who amount to some 160,000 people aged 8 to 80 years, what they think are the factors which help them to learn and he captured this on questionnaires. Phil has actually asked far more people than many highly respected learning theorists did when building their learning theories. He rightly suggests that such a volume of answers, collected from the use of his own self-devised questionnaires, carries some conviction from a wide cross-section of ages and cultures. When analysed for a recent edition of Phil's well-known book about teaching, the responses grouped around 'seven factors underpinning successful learning' (Race, 2014: 26). These are:

- wanting to learn
- needing to learn
- learning by doing
- learning through feedback
- making sense
- verbalizing orally
- learning through assessing.

(Continued)

(Continued)

Phil represents these in his work and writings as an interconnected cycle of factors, advising that 'they don't necessarily follow on from each other in a particular order', but that they 'all affect each other, and may all occur simultaneously and concurrently'. He suggests these factors are like 'ripples on a pond' when a pebble is dropped in it (Race, 2014: 40). Phil doesn't describe this as a learning theory, but it is an example which fits well with and underlines the proposition in this chapter that teachers understand their students better when they think more deeply about how they learn. It also suggests that Phil has signed up to at least some of the professional values argued for at the beginning of this chapter. You will also notice that the factors involved are all strikingly human and people-centred (apart from, perhaps, 'learning through assessment'). Even that factor has a very human dimension. In my experience, when assessment is fair, open and accessible and students understand how it can help them to learn, they actually enjoy having their learning assessed.

Learning theories to enrich learning and teaching

Carl Rogers – becoming a person

What are Carl Rogers' key ideas about learning?

Carl Rogers (1902–1987) has been described as 'the most important psychologist in American history' (Kirschenbaum and Henderson, 1990: xi) and as a 'quiet revolutionary' (xiv). His ideas have influenced many teachers and many others working with people for many years.

His work led him to believe that, as human beings, 'all individuals have within themselves the ability to guide their own lives in a manner which is both personally satisfying and socially constructive' (Rogers, 1961: 14). This approach instantly moves the emphasis away from the professional working with people, and towards the people themselves, and Rogers believed that people were very much able to decide their own actions for themselves, and follow them through. For Rogers, genuine learning is

learning which is more than an accumulation of facts. It is learning which makes a difference – in the individual's behaviour, in the course of action he chooses for the future, in his attitudes and in his personality. It is a pervasive learning which is not just an accretion of knowledge, but which interpenetrates with every portion of his existence' (Rogers, 1961: 280).

The way in which teaching can help this learning take place is through a 'helping relationship'. 'In a particular type of helping relationship, we free the individuals to find their inner wisdom and confidence, and they will make increasingly healthier and more constructive choices' (Rogers, 1990: 14).

Rogers' core conditions for a helping relationship

In order for this helping relationship to work in an educational context, there need to be certain 'qualities that facilitate learning' present in the teacher, or 'core conditions' involved, and these are:

- *Realness in the facilitator of learning* – To put this at its most simple, this is about the teacher being a real person who develops a helping relationship with students in an open way, with no pretence or façade based on who they are. The emphasis on the teaching context is on being yourself in a way that makes your interaction with students natural and genuine.

- *Prizing, acceptance, trust* – This condition is about seeing the learner as a valued fellow human being, with their own worth and flaws but also their own capacity and natural inclination to learn and change. Once that prizing, acceptance and trust is established, the best chance of a helping relationship is in place.

- *Empathetic understanding* – This is explained well with Rogers' own words when he states that 'students feel deeply appreciative when they are simply understood – not evaluated, not judged, simply understood from their own point of view, not the teacher's. (Rogers, 1990: 304–311)

Underlying these core conditions for the teacher is what Rogers (205) described as 'unconditional positive regard' for students and colleagues alike, or starting from the position that all people deserve to be treated as valued and with respect irrespective of their situation, views or previous experience. The helping relationship is essential in encouraging students to feel that their experience is both understood and respected, and this literally helps them to learn, but does not control how they do it. Creating an environment in which your students learn becomes one of the key functions of the teacher, rather than transmitting learning to them. Rogers accepts that this more open approach to teaching is demanding in terms of preparation as the teacher is never as sure of what learning may take place, as can be the case in more traditional teacher-centred approaches. Rogers was himself a very good teacher, and did spend considerable time preparing to support his students' learning.

The research used to develop Rogers' learning theories

Rogers refined and developed his theories on an ongoing basis over many years. He worked as a psychologist and teacher for over 50 years, and consistently undertook research into his methods and approaches throughout that time, and drew on much research from others. Research undertaken or used by Rogers involved a variety of methods, many thousands of people, and took account of studies on topics such as influences on the behaviour of children; relationships with individuals in therapeutic and counselling work; and the personalities and attitudes of teachers and the influence of this on student learning.

Critiques of Rogers' theories

Rogers' ideas have their critics, and it has been suggested that the closeness he envisions between the teacher and the student can make the integrity of the subject, and the boundaries between the teacher and the student blurred and potentially problematic (Smith, 2004). There is also potentially a danger in underestimating the value which can be achieved by other direct and more teacher-centred methods of teaching. Information transmission and its reception by students does have a place in learning, and can be a crucial component of the helping relationship.

Relevance to people-centred teaching

Rogers' methods and ideas are still used widely in teaching and research today, and a search in 2017 among books, research papers and studies where the authors are using his methods finds thousands of papers, articles and publications. Rogers' own particular type of people-centred teaching still resonates with many in education, and research reports positive learning gains from the use of his approaches and methods. His suggestions for forging the relationships we as teachers can and should develop with our students to help the learning process, and the techniques which can be used to make that relationship helpful are also of great value.

Teaching using Carl Rogers' ideas

A review of research which made use of Carl Rogers' ideas about creating a positive 'classroom climate' was published by the (now defunct) school-based General Teaching Council in 2008. As part of the 'Research for Teachers' series (GTC, 2008) this review found substantial evidence to confirm the impact of this important aspect of his thinking. The publication reviewed evidence and cited research indicating that the use of Rogers' more student-centred approaches:

- reduced student absence
- increased student self-concept and self-esteem
- increased academic achievement
- increased spontaneity and the use of higher level thinking

Act of connection - how is your 'classroom climate'?

Give honest answers to the following questions

- How much do your students talk in your teaching sessions, and how much do you listen?
- How would you describe your 'classroom climate'?
- Is it emotionally supportive for all, and do you have a helping relationship with your students?
- How does this make a difference?

If you believe any of your answers leave room for improvement, make plans to change the way you establish and manage your own classroom climate to meet Rogers' core conditions.

Etienne Wenger – learning as participation in communities of practice

What are Wenger's key ideas about learning?

As has already featured in Chapter 1, Etienne Wenger (1952–) developed (working with Jean Lave) ideas about learning as a social activity taking place in groups, and critiqued how education systems tend to be based on individuals and their learning. He asks key questions of this approach:

> What if we adopted a different perspective, one that placed learning in the context of our lived experience of participation in the world?
>
> What if we assumed that learning is as much a part of human nature as eating or sleeping, that it is both life-sustaining and inevitable, and that – given a chance – we are quite good at it?
>
> What if, in addition, we assumed that learning is, in its essence, a fundamentally social phenomenon, reflecting our own deeply social nature as human beings capable of knowing? (Wenger, 2010: 209)

Wenger is a thinker who acknowledges that 'there are many different kinds of learning theory. Each emphasizes different aspects of learning, and each is therefore useful for different purposes' (2010: 209).

Four key assumptions are at the heart of his ideas about learning, and they are:

- Humans are social beings and this is central to their learning.

- Knowledge is about achieving competence in the aspects of living, learning and working which we value, such as 'singing in tune, fixing machines, writing poetry, being convivial, growing up as a boy or a girl' (2010: 209).

- Knowing is about participating in the pursuit of those competencies, that is, 'of active engagement in the world' (2010: 209).

- Meaning is about how we experience the world and engage with it. The way in which that becomes meaningful is the learning which is produced.

Wenger sums up what he considers to be the 'primary focus of this theory' as being 'on learning as social participation. Participation here refers not just to local events of engagement in certain activities with certain people, but to a more encompassing process of being active participants in the practices of social communities and constructing identities in relation to these communities' (2010: 209).

These ideas move beyond Rogers' more individually-centred theorising and out into a broader concept which has been seen as being about 'learning communities'.

The research used to develop Wenger's learning theories

Anthropologist Jean Lave and Etienne Wenger coined the term 'community of practice' while studying apprenticeship as a learning model. They carried out observations of apprenticeships including Yucatec midwives, Vai and Gola tailors, US Navy quartermasters, meat-cutters, and non-drinking alcoholics in Alcoholics Anonymous. They found that people tended to start at the edge or periphery of groups, and moved further into the centre of group activities as they became more confident. As a result of this work and other associated research, they concluded that learning is a process of social participation, rather than an individual acquisition of knowledge.

Critiques of Wenger's theories

Firstly it has been pointed out that communities of practice do not always function effectively, and that this can be because of power relationships, difficulties participants have in the levels of participation needed, and barriers which can prevent people from entering these communities

(Avis et al. 2002; Roberts, 2006). It is, of course, also the case that the individual can experience new and positive learning without a community of practice. As we have said already, Wenger himself did not claim his learning theory was the only one which works.

Relevance to people-centred teaching

People-centred teachers can make use of this approach to learning in a number of ways. Helping students to become a 'community of learning' is one way. A community of learning is a group of students who work together on an ongoing basis on a shared activity, problem, interest or topic to develop and deepen their understanding of it. They value the participation in the activity and work in ways which help solve problems and develop thinking, ideas and actions. Wenger's term is 'communities of practice' and these already take place through shared interests and experiences in many ways in our communities. Book clubs, sports clubs and groups based on hobbies are all examples, and there can also be less wholesome activities such as membership of gangs. At least some of your students will already be engaged in such activity, so developing a community of learning of students for your own teaching can be very positive. The use of technology and particularly social media can be powerful in both cementing and fragmenting such communities and communities of practice. This is explored further in Chapter 5.

 *Spotlight on pedagogy*

Communities of practice for FE?

Taking part with other teachers in a community of practice can help all four of the connections of the connected professional. The process of communication and working together is helpful for the networked connection; the themes and topics addressed are likely to be relevant to the practical con- nection and the democratic and civic connections can be present within the community processes and the range of participants included in that community. There have however been barriers when communities of practice have been promoted in FE. The ideas from Etienne Wenger do have ready associations with the development of organisations and potential benefits for learning and develop- ment within those organisations. FE organisations have however found it problematic to accommo- date the approaches and ideas involved as they invest autonomy in the groups of practitioners, and could be seen to threaten existing hierarchies. Research by Avis et al. suggests that the prevalence in FE of 'a top-down managerialism that is distanced from the sorts of dialogue embedded in the notion of a community of practice' (2002: 31) militates against their formation. This does not however mean that it is impossible to make use of Wenger's excellent ideas.

 *Reflective learning exercise*

An example of teaching with Etienne Wenger's ideas

There are many examples of the successful development and use of communities of practice for and by teachers and other professionals. There are examples of student communities of learning such as McQueen et al. (2014). A group of HE practitioners made use of an online peer working tool which is designed to encourage collaboration to support coursework for biology students. One cohort of students (some 300 in total) were firstly given training and support from their teachers, then made use of an online tool (called PeerWise and widely used in HE) to engage with each other and the course content, collaborate and undertake self-marking, peer marking and give peer feedback. The teaching staff specifically used Wenger's ideas to help them develop and establish the ways in which the community of learning could take place. The results included positive feedback about the online tool and evidence of deeper understanding from the students, and increased performance in a range of types of assessment. McQueen et al. found that the 'effective engagement of our students associates positively and significantly with high performance not only in the multiple-choice component of the course but with course-work, exam essay, exam problem and overall course marks' (2014: 372).

Reflective learning exercise

Act of connection - creating a community of learning with your students

To start to create a community of learning with your own students, use this activity:

- Early in your course, ask the students to devise some short ground rules for the work you all do together in discussions, group work and other in-session activities.
- Select a work in progress, such as ongoing preparation for an assessment, which all students need to complete.
- Ask your students to share their own progress, ideas and challenges for the piece of work, and to produce a short list of helpful tips for all students.
- Ask your students to agree a regular process for ensuring their collaborative work is shared by all for all.
- Share this first list across the group to all group members before the next session.
- Start the next session with that list.

Abraham Maslow – human needs and self-actualisation

What are Abraham Maslow's key ideas about learning?

Abraham Maslow (1908–1970) is one of the most familiar and (in terms of teachers applying his thinking to their own teaching) most understood learning theorists for teachers in FE. His philosophy can be summed up by his statement that 'what a man can be, he must be. This we will call self-actualisation' (Maslow, 1954: 93). He is best known for his 'hierarchy of needs', usually represented as a pyramid (see Figure 2.1), which displays the physiological and psychological needs that he argued must be met for people to achieve self-actualisation, or the place in a person's life where they have achieved the best they can be, and realised their potential. At the bottom of the pyramid are the basic 'physiological needs' such as hunger, thirst, warmth and rest. These are followed by 'safety needs' such as security, stability and protection, then 'social needs' such as the need to belong, love, friendship and family. The penultimate stage in the hierarchy of needs is 'esteem

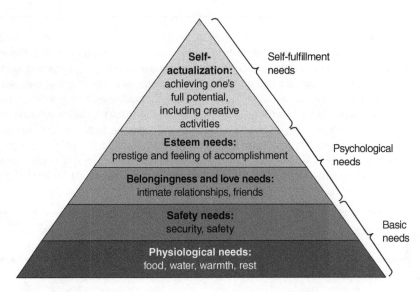

Figure 2.1 Maslow's hierarchy of needs

needs', and this includes self-esteem, confidence, achievement and respect of and by others. The final stage at the apex of the pyramid is 'self-actualisation' which includes problem solving, creativity, morality and achieving one's full potential.

The research used to develop Maslow's learning theories

Maslow's ideas have been hugely influential, and he developed them over a period of time from the 1940s to 1970 when he died from a heart attack. He carried out and made use of biographical studies of mainly healthy individuals, which was unusual at the time, in a search for answers about the factors which motivated people, and what he described as the essence of people's lives, rather than carrying out a series of scientific experiments. One of his main studies used in the development of his theory of motivation was small, including only around 20 people, selected by Maslow himself. He studied them and their writings. The subjects were all people who Maslow considered to be self-actualised individuals.

Critiques of Maslow's theories

Despite their major influence, Maslow's research methods have been widely criticised, as have a number of his key ideas. His approach was seen as elitist, and the individuals he chose to include in his study were often not average members of society with ordinary jobs or purposes (Pearson, 1999). There have also been suggestions that he chose subjects who he believed would fit with the conclusions he had already come to, and that his sample was biased. The hierarchical and somewhat fixed nature of the pyramid and the categorisation of the needs involved, and the lack of life situations which were mixed across the levels of the hierarchy have also been argued to be weaknesses in his work. For example someone who lives in poverty and physical discomfort may well still experience love and belonging, and may indeed achieve a degree of self-actualisation despite some of their lower order needs not having been met (Aubrey and Riley, 2015).

Maslow's relevance to people-centred teaching

Despite these well-founded critiques, the core of Maslow's message about humans as naturally inclined towards self-actualisation appears to ring true with many teachers, who have, in my experience, been ready to apply his ideas in their teaching. Most people become teachers because they want to help people succeed with their learning, and to achieve to their full potential. The very useful thing about Maslow's theory of motivation is that it provides a series of steps which, although flawed, clearly do have relevance to the process of learning and the practice of teaching. If your students are in a room with poor heating, poor furniture, poor surroundings, and there are limited resources to provide for their learning, and some of them arrive hungry, tired and grumpy, this is not exactly a situation which is conducive to learning. As their teacher, you would be faced with this situation before any attempt at teaching has taken place. It is amazing how motivation can still develop under particularly difficult circumstances, and one of a teacher's key roles is to help with developing and maintaining it.

 Spotlight on pedagogy

Teaching with Abraham Maslow's ideas

Research about motivating learners in FE

Susan Wallace (2014: 346) published findings from a research project which sought to 'investigate teachers' strategies for motivating learners and managing non-compliant behaviour in the further education sector.' It involved 203 FE teachers and catalogued learner behaviours 'most commonly identified by teachers as "challenging", and the methods teachers employ to successfully address these.' The study found a significant lack of motivation across the 16–19 age group, and some evidence that 'a positive teacher-learner relationship is a major factor in the motivation to learn' (2014: 358). The evidence about the impact of strategies used to motivate students was not conclusive, but there were 'indications that teachers had most success in building student motivation and encouraging positive behaviour in cases where the relationship between teachers and learners appeared positive, cheerful and mutually respectful' (2014: 358). Wallace argued that these findings appear to reflect 'humanist theories of learning associated with Maslow (1987) and Rogers (1983), which argue that students' more basic needs – for acceptance and a sense of belonging, for example – must be met before they can engage with the business of learning' (2014: 358).

 Reflective learning exercise

Act of connection – are you self-actualised?

As always, when working on activities that consider needs and feelings, be aware of the potential for negative feelings and emotions to emerge as well as positive ones. Firstly talk through Maslow's theory with your students and be sure they have absorbed it enough to apply it to their own situations. Each student is going to produce a 'self-actualisation tracker' over the course of a week (and so are you).

(Continued)

(Continued)

- Give a hard copy of a diagram of Maslow's hierarchy of needs with space for notes on the same handout (the pyramid usually works well) to each student.
- Ask them to annotate the diagram during the coming week with comments or emojis (small images such as smileys used in electronic messages and Web pages) about which needs have or have not been met, and when and where that has taken place. (For example a session in a cold uncomfortable room was not good at meeting physical needs could be noted as 'cold in room xxxx on Monday ☹'.)
- Keep your own self-actualisation tracker, annotating it with your thoughts on how your teaching may, or may not have helped meet any of Maslow's hierarchy of needs over the same period of a week. (For example 'my Thursday students did a group presentation which really seemed to boost their self-esteem ☺'.)
- When you are next together with the group, share the results (including yours) and discuss the entries, what can be learned from them, and what improvements could be made.
- Make a list of agreed action points which you can then circulate to the students and review in future sessions.

Ken Robinson – building the future through creativity

What are Ken Robinson's key ideas about learning?

Ken Robinson (1950 –) is one of the best known global figures in education today, and he has carried out research, produced significant numbers of publications, advised organisations and governments and talked and taught around the world about education (including featuring in one of the most watched TED talks of all time at https://www.ted.com/talks/ken_robinson_says_schools_kill_creativity/up-next). He is not necessarily known as, nor does he advertise himself as a learning theorist, but I have included him here as his thinking on education and creativity is striking, engaging and thought-provoking (and of course highly relevant to people-centred teaching).

 Spotlight on pedagogy

Ken Robinson and creativity – key ideas

Robinson's key ideas align well with the other theorists discussed so far in this chapter. He emphasises the human nature of learning and education when he states that his 'starting point is that everyone has huge creative capacities as a natural result of being a human being. The challenge is to develop them. A culture of creativity has to involve everybody not just a select few' (Robinson, 2011: 4). His work is aimed at helping individuals 'understand the depth of their creative abilities and why they might have doubted them' and to 'encourage organisations, particularly those in education to believe in their students' 'powers of innovation and to create the conditions where they will flourish' (2011: xvi). Robinson's cites three reasons for his ideas and these are

- 'The ways in which we all live, learn and experience life are shaped by the ideas, beliefs and values of human imagination and culture' and this creates a world which 'is created out of our minds as much as from the natural environment' (2011: xvi).

- The environment in which we fulfil our creative potential needs to be one which encourages us and this includes its physical design, organisational structure, and degree of creative culture.

- Systems for organising education need to change.

Robinson laments the degree to which educational policy and educational systems are pervaded by 'a kind of mania' which is often not at all conducive to creativity. He does not argue, as some suggest, that this is because teachers are not creative, but that government and others involved in managing education systems create environments and structures which stifle that creativity. This results in education often supporting the creative human side of learning despite, rather than because of, the organisational system and culture in which it is located.

Robinson proposes a series of principles which he argues could help education change, and they include:

- Education should go 'back to basics' (Robinson, 2011: 247) by ensuring that the relationship between teacher and student, the most important part of education, is the primary organising goal in our quest 'to improve the quality of students' learning' (2011: 249).

- Developing the 'individual talents and sensibilities' (2011: 249) of students in combination with a recognition of the need to 'broaden and stretch' (2011: 250).

- Learning in educational establishments should engage with and interact directly with the world outside school, including working in the community.

- Success creates success. 'When students find something they enjoy and can excel in, they do better in education generally' (2011: 256).

- Creativity is for everyone. 'Creativity is possible in every discipline and should be promoted throughout the world of education' (2011: 256).

The research used to develop Ken Robinson's learning theories

In his publications and the development of his ideas, Robinson makes use of much published research on the brain, especially some of the recent research into the ways the brain works. He also makes use of studies of environments, approaches, organisations and localities where creativity has been prioritised and evaluated in building and developing his arguments. He also utilises the work of other thinkers including Rogers and Maslow. He has headed national reviews focused on creativity in education which have summarised research as part of their objectives, and is still very active at the time of writing.

Critiques of Ken Robinson's theories

It can be argued that the link between creativity as an essential aspect of developing human potential is present in the available evidence, but that there are other essential factors also involved which do not emphasise creativity as much but which still could be valid solutions (Buckingham and Jones, 2001). There is also the ongoing discussion which is simply put as innate talent versus the value of practice.

Examples are cited in this argument of people across history who did not demonstrate innate creative talent, but developed it through continuous practice. There are also criticisms that his work exaggerates the degree to which creativity is stifled in education and that this is not a genuine reflection of reality (Munday, 2014). As a teacher in FE, you are best placed to judge how much creative approaches are or are not valued.

Relevance to people-centred teaching

Robinson's emphasis on creativity as a central trait of humanity, and one which helps all aspects of society, work, learning and living does, as has already been said, resonate strongly with the principles and values of people-centred teaching. Robinson was the chair of a 'National Advisory Committee on Creative and Cultural Education' (about schools only of course) which reported in 2001, and the report described 'creative education' as education which develops 'capacities for original ideas and action' and that this is the key to unlocking potential and that 'Britain's economic prosperity and social cohesion depend on this' (Robinson, 2001: 5). The Robinson report also argued that teachers should use 'imaginative approaches to make learning more interesting, exciting and effective', and that there are 'three related tasks in teaching for creativity: encouraging, identifying and fostering' (2001: 102–103). Ideas such as these are clearly relevant to the notion of people-centred teaching, and provide further support for it as an approach.

 *Spotlight on pedagogy*

Teaching with Ken Robinson's ideas

An Ofsted report on 44 schools and how they used 'creative approaches' (Ofsted, 2010) supports some of Robinson's recommended approaches, and is certainly relevant to FE. The report found that pupils who were taught in ways which 'encouraged questioning, debate, experimentation, presentation and critical reflection enjoyed the challenge, and had a sense of personal achievement' (2010: 5). The success of creative approaches was closely related to 'a whole-school agenda to disseminate and embed creative approaches to learning.' Approaches developed in creative subjects became embedded in other subjects such as science and mathematics, and 'schools in challenging circumstances . . . showed the greatest improvements' (2010: 4). Ofsted importantly concluded that the examples of creative approaches 'were accompanied by better than average achievement and standards, or a marked upward trend' (2010: 5).

 *Reflective learning exercise*

Act of connection – drawing an idea

This is a really straightforward starter and creative thinking activity which can help to unlock creative ideas and feelings in a simple and fun way. You will need a supply of flip chart paper and good pens to write and draw on it.

- In groups of about 4-5 students, ask them to draw a picture of their version of an idea, concept or topic relevant in their course. For example, draw 'a community' or 'health and safety' or 'Shakespeare's sonnets'.
- They need to be given a fixed time (e.g. 15 minutes) to complete the activity.
- Students will need to at least think about how they are going to agree what to draw, and who is going to draw it, then whether they are going to draw an image, a scene, and how or if they wish to label their image.
- Once all images have been drawn, they should all be shared as a 'gallery of ideas', and a digital photo taken of each flip chart.
- Comparing what they came up with is best done during the same session, but can also be effective during another session, using the digital photos to prompt discussion.
- When linked with topics on your course, this can work really well to produce more open and creative ideas.

Katherine Weare – warm, healthy learning relationships

What are Katherine Weare's key ideas about learning?

Katherine Weare (1950 –) is a professor of education who has researched and written widely in the areas of mental health and emotional and social well-being in schools. Her work is based in schools, and has influenced education policy in the UK and beyond, but it is again relevant to other sectors of education. Weare advocates the 'ultimate aim' of her work as to 'help produce more socially minded citizens, who see the benefit of participating in social and community processes, increased levels of social capital (a feeling of belonging to a community), a more flexible, resilient and effective workforce and a reduction in violence and crime' (2004: 15–16). Her thinking is therefore highly relevant to this book, and can be applied in FE. The focus taken in this chapter is on her work around the 'learning relationships' which can help students to achieve 'emotional literacy'. Weare defines emotional literacy 'for the individual' as 'the ability to understand ourselves and other people, and in particular to be aware of, understand, and use information about the emotional states of ourselves and others with competence. It includes the ability to understand, express and manage our own emotions, and respond to the emotions of others, in ways that are helpful to ourselves and others' (Weare, 2004: 2).

For organisations to properly support the emotional literacy of their students, they need to adopt a whole organisation approach, and ensure that their staff are trained in the competences needed. Weare cites research to argue that it has been concluded 'unequivocally that whole-school approaches are essential when attempting to tackle emotional and social issues' (Weare, 2004: 53). Weare also echoes ideas from Rogers when stating that students' emotional literacy is fostered by 'warm, personal, trustworthy relationships' which are 'fundamental for the growth of self-esteem' (2004: 85). Teachers need, as we have seen argued by many of our theorists, to have 'good relationship skills' (2004: 131) and these relationships are 'a key factor in producing high levels of staff and pupil morale and performance' (2004: 41).

The research used to develop Katherine Weare's learning theories

Katherine Weare has worked for the World Health Organization, the European Union and as an advisor for the UK government on social and emotional learning. Her work has included reviewing educational provision at home and abroad, and related research. This has led to an approach to social and emotional learning (SEL) which has been adopted by a significant number of English primary schools. She has reviewed and researched evidence in this field comprehensively and particularly recommends engaging the whole community inside and outside educational establishments in the process of supporting their educational organisation and its students.

Critiques of Katherine Weare's theories

As has been the case to some degree with critiques of Ken Robinson, it has been argued that research about emotional intelligence and emotional literacy does not as convincingly confirm its value and impact as is claimed (Barchard, 2003). There is also some criticism of taking the ideas and turning them into a learning programme for all students, which is partially what has happened in primary schools as a result of Weare's work. This critique asserts the reasonable position that what happens in school may well be a very significant part of life, especially in younger years, but it is not the only part of life, and outside educational influences need to be more recognised and accommodated (Matthews et al., 2004).

Relevance to people-centred teaching

The focus for Weare is particularly in mental health within social well-being and emotional literacy, and this gives another twist to the theories which are relevant to people-centred teaching. The whole community approach links well with the 'democratic connection' with its emphasis on professionals working together and the 'civic connection' for the close relationship with the broader community. Weare's ideas also resonate well with the professional values outlined at the start of this chapter.

Spotlight on pedagogy

Teaching with Katherine Weare's ideas

A small study of 35 vocational FE students considering the presence of approaches and interventions which fostered 'flow' for students was carried out by Tarling (2016). He considered which teaching strategies and interventions indicated a good level of incidences of 'flow' or levels of enjoyment and engagement in their learning which immersed them in the learning activity 'to the exclusion of everything else' (Tarling, 2016: 303). The evidence of the small study was analysed with the help of Weare's approaches and indicated the key element from the teaching perspective was the way in which the teachers had facilitated and enabled a positive and supportive learning environment which was clearly socially and emotionally rewarding and motivating for the students concerned. The researcher argued that the key implications for teaching were to build trust with the students and their self-confidence early in their courses, so that they could further develop independence within their own vocational learning. This was not about direct teaching, but about the people-centred relationship with teachers and their peers which fostered confidence and well-being.

Reflective learning exercise

Act of connection – how emotionally literate are you, your students and your organisation?

Combine these questions in any way you wish to use them, either with colleagues or students. You will need to explain what emotional literacy is about first.

- How emotionally literate are you?
- How emotionally literate are your (fellow) students?
- How confident are you about helping your (fellow) students develop their emotional literacy?
- How emotionally literate is your organisation?

Use the answers to discuss strategies and actions which could build emotional literacy for all.

bell hooks – education as the practice of freedom

What are bell hooks' key ideas about learning?

bell hooks (1952 –) is a social activist, feminist, author and educator from the USA. She adopted the name bell hooks as a tribute to her great grandmother Bell Blair Hooks, and is a significant thinker about progressive and democratic education. Her key ideas as discussed here focus around education's capacity to contribute to reduce the inequalities which still exist for many people in matters associated with race, gender and social class.

bell hooks' educational writings and thinking focus on the notion that education offers us hope, and that

> My hope emerges from those places of struggle where I witness individuals positively transforming their lives and the world around them. Educating is always a vocation rooted in hopefulness. As teachers we believe that learning is possible, that nothing can keep an open mind from seeking after knowledge and finding a way to know (hooks, 2003: xiv).

She coined the term 'transformative pedagogy' (hooks, 1994: 39) for her approaches to teaching and learning. We can see some of her similarities to other thinkers from this chapter when she argues that teaching should be carried out 'in a manner that respects and cares for the souls of our students', and that 'teachers must be actively involved; committed to a process of self-actualization that promotes their own well-being if they are to teach in a manner that empowers students' (hooks, 1994: 13 and 15). hooks is even brave enough to argue that our teaching spaces ought to be places of joy where enjoyment and achievement are part of the 'location of possibility' where we 'labour for freedom' (hooks, 1994: 207). She is a thinker who can inspire, when sharing her own hopes that 'in that field of possibility we have the opportunity to labour for freedom, to demand of ourselves and our comrades, an openness of mind and heart that allows us to face reality even as we collectively imagine ways to move beyond boundaries, to transgress. This is education as the practice of freedom' (hooks 1994: 207).

The research used to develop bell hooks' learning theories

As a black writer who has written about the black female in US culture and inequality in all its forms, hooks develops her ideas using her own personal experiences about how she has been influenced by teachers at school and university, and also her own experiences as a teacher (not all of which by any means are positive). She develops and expresses her ideas through reflection on her life experiences rather than empirical research, and adopts a personal and open style which is different to some of the educational thinkers featured in this chapter. She is strongly influenced by thinkers such as Paolo Freire, and her ideas link to other thinkers and theorists such as Dewey.

Critiques of bell hooks' theories

hooks has been criticised for not having taken a more scholarly approach to her work (Pettis, 1986) (she does have an MA awarded in 1976, and a PhD awarded in 1983) but she writes with a powerful conviction, authority and passion. She has also been accused of taking a too emotional approach and tone in her writings, where she promotes love, spirituality and imagination as key components of teaching (Shelly, 1995). For many, that makes her even more relevant and meaningful.

Relevance to people-centred teaching

Another critique of bell hooks is that she has not provided clear practical advice about how to use her philosophy and approaches to teaching as a teacher (Lacom and Hadley, 2009). She may not provide a step-by-step guide or toolkit (thank goodness), but her 'practical wisdom' includes references to active student learning, supporting and building confidence in students and the importance of student voice and experience. People-centred teaching is about emotion and humanity just as much as it is about learning, so hooks' focus is another directly helpful and relevant set of ideas. Her thinking relates very directly to the democratic and civic connections of the connected professional, and she readily emphasises the need for the practical connection for the techniques needed to be able to realise the democratic and civic visions.

 *Spotlight on pedagogy*

Teaching with bell hooks' ideas

An imaginative higher education research project in the Creative Media and Digital Culture Program of Washington State University in Vancouver was established and operated using hooks' ideas of 'transformative pedagogy'. This included approaches designed to use student-centred, holistic and practice-oriented approaches 'that allow students to create their own knowledge' (Grigar, 2013: 1). The teaching team involved firstly spent time clarifying their own philosophy of 'digital technology' and created key principles on which to base the curriculum development and teaching, which were open, democratic and student-centred and which used the best pedagogical principles relating to the educational uses of technology. These principles were built into the teaching by using an 'active, engaged approach to learning' with a 'focus on the uniqueness of the individual and heavy emphasis on ethics' (Grigar, 2013: 1). Another important part of the hooks approach is to ensure that the creation of real items is part of the learning activity, and this was also built in. hooks also argues that learning should have a community engagement focus (the civic connection again) and a 'focus in helping others through a community outreach approach' (Grigar, 2013: 1) was also designed into the course. The results of this use of hooks' ideas were impressive and included students working on collaborative mobile learning projects with local companies, then gaining employment with them; working with local community groups on projects; the creation of student fellows within the digital technology programme; the embedding of these principles in a range of courses at the university, and a number of teaching and student awards.

 Reflective learning exercise

Act of connection - students influencing their future

The emphasis with this activity is on giving students firstly the confidence to think about and share their 'life stories', and then to connect them with some personal relevance to the topic or subject you are teaching them. Education is always a good starting point.

Ask your students to:

- Think about and/or note down/draw what the topic has meant for them in their lives so far (you could use almost any topic here – the subject you are teaching; the place where students live; their hobbies or interests).
- Reflect on what actions, feelings and ideas have influenced that process.
- Share the results with at least one other person in your group.

Then for general discussion

- What does this tell us about how our lives are made?
- What steps can we take to influence our own futures?

This kind of activity needs to take place regularly and the approaches concerned need to be built into your teaching on an ongoing basis to have maximum impact.

This chapter

This chapter opened with a set of professional values for all teachers in FE, and then introduced six thinkers about education, the learning theories associated with them and their relevance to people-centred teaching and learning. They were Carl Rogers, Etienne Wenger, Abraham Maslow, Ken Robinson, Katherine Weare and bell hooks. Each thinker's theoretical ideas were introduced, the key points explained, along with an indication of where the ideas came from and a summary of critiques of the theories. A range of spotlights on pedagogy and reflective learning exercises provide many opportunities to showcase the ideas in practice, and to give you a chance to try them out.

I hope that this chapter has shown you that there are many people-centred learning theories which research has shown do work in practice, and which are well worth your making use of. I find a number of them inspiring and they fill me with positivity and hope when I try them out. I hope they can do the same for you.

Further reading notes

hooks, bell (1994) Teaching to Transgress. Education as the practice of freedom. London: Routledge.

If you want to read a publication by someone who is passionate about education and can communicate both her ideas and that passion in a way which is readable and inspiring, read some of the essays in this book. Chapters include:

- Engaged Pedagogy
- Embracing Change: Teaching in a Multicultural World
- Theory as Liberatory Practice
- Building a Teaching Community: A Dialogue
- Confronting Class in the Classroom

www.learning-theories.com

This is another 'must visit' website. Its home page invitation goes as follows:

> 'Are you a student or teacher? Explore our easy-to-read summaries of learning theories, educational guides and useful tools below.'

The site provides this very well, and includes many theories and theorists, which are grouped in various ways.

Rogers, C. R. (1990) *The Carl Rogers Reader*. Kirschenbaum, H. and Land Henderson, V. (eds). London: Constable.

This selection of Rogers' writings is as good a one volume compendium of his ideas in his own words that you will get. You should easily be able to get it second hand and some sections will be available via Google books. Reading the ideas as he wrote them makes his work come alive, so this text is thoroughly recommended.

National Standards which are addressed by this chapter are:

1. Reflect on what works best in your teaching and learning to meet the diverse needs of learners.

2. Evaluate and challenge your practice, values and beliefs.

3. Inspire, motivate and raise aspirations of learners through your enthusiasm and knowledge.

4. Be creative and innovative in selecting and adapting strategies to help learners to learn.

5. Value and promote social and cultural diversity, equality of opportunity and inclusion.

6. Build positive and collaborative relationships with colleagues and learners.

9. Apply theoretical understanding of effective practice in teaching, learning and assessment drawing on research and other evidence.

13. Motivate and inspire learners to promote achievement and develop their skills to enable progression.

Part 2

Just teach

Chapter 3

Just teach 1 – Building and keeping trust

 Key learning points in this chapter

Building trust

What evidence is there that building trust works?

Building trust with colleagues

Golden moments and troubled times

Weare (2004: 10) advises that we should 'build up trust' as 'the bedrock of [learning] relationships'. This chapter provides more details on the approaches and practical strategies for building trust between teachers and students, between and among students, and between teachers and other teachers. This is the anchor of people-centred teaching and the techniques involved are central to the practical connection of a connected professional.

Building trust

Building trust with your students includes developing empathy, positive use of emotions, establishing and supporting positive self-concepts and engaging positive motivation. Building trust will help support participation in 'acts of connection' and can help our students to achieve 'golden moments'. That same trust can also help us to remember (if we needed a reminder) that we all (students included) have bad days, or 'troubled times' but that trust can help us all to better manage and survive the bad days. Also crucially, if the learners can't trust the teacher, they are less likely to take the risks or accept the challenges which lead to successful learning.

Spotlight on pedagogy

Rogers' core conditions that facilitate learning

Let's firstly remind ourselves of Carl Rogers' core conditions that facilitate learning. They are realness in the facilitator of learning; prizing, acceptance, trust; and empathic understanding. These are the 'attitudinal qualities that exist in the personal relationship between the facilitator and the learner' (Rogers, 1990: 305). To demonstrate those qualities you need to be able to:

- show yourself as a person to your students, not a distant figure
- respect, accept and value each of your students as a worthwhile human being, faults and all
- actively show that you are aware of, take account of and understand how your students feel, and what it is like to be in their shoes.

Some teachers will naturally possess some or all of these qualities, and others may not. I hope you have some of them, as teaching will be hard going without them! It is possible, with training and support, to develop and learn the skills and understanding needed to build trust with your students, and the next section of this chapter provides examples and activities to help that process.

Spotlight on pedagogy

The skilled helper – Gerard Egan

Gerard Egan is a professor of organization studies and psychology at Loyola University of Chicago. He describes the skills we as professionals need when supporting other people as 'helping skills'. Egan was influenced by Carl Rogers, and produced some really useful ideas and practical guidance which can help us to build a trusting learning relationship with our students. Egan (1994) produced a 'three stage model of helping', and the three stages are:

1 Exploration – where am I now?
2 New understanding – where would I like to be?
3 Action – how can I get there?

To successfully achieve your potential, Egan argues that you need to move through these three stages constantly, although you may not always successfully negotiate all of them every time. As a teacher, you can help your students to progress through these stages, but you need 'helping skills' to do so, and these are:

- Attending – showing visibly that you are paying attention to your students as individuals and as a group. This can involve making eye contact, being relaxed with them and making use of positive body language.

- Active listening - paying close attention to, and acknowledging the thoughts and feelings of your students.

- Reflecting - mirroring what your students are feeling in a way which helps them to recognise the consequences of their thoughts and feelings.

- Encouraging - actively helping your students to think for and understand themselves.

- Questioning - asking questions which will clarify and help students to focus on making their own choices and decisions, and acknowledging the possible consequences.

Developing helping skills – two examples

Active listening

When you are talking something over with your students, you can help first of all by really listening to what they have to say. By giving your full attention to that individual person, and concentrating on what they are saying, you help them to feel accepted and understood. This way of listening also stops you from taking on the burden of trying to find answers for them. Active listening is very different from normal social conversation, where we are often waiting for someone else to finish talking while planning what we are going to say next – and are mostly failing to hear what is being said in the meantime! This is quite often acceptable in everyday circumstances, but when someone is worried or unhappy, it can leave them feeling frustrated, left out, or even rejected. Really listening carefully to another person needs a great deal of concentration, and if you are thinking hard about your responses, only part of what they are saying can be taken in. So you need to try to hold back your own thoughts and judgements while listening, which is not always easy. The next act of connection gives you an idea of how difficult it can be, but also of how it is possible to learn active listening.

 *Reflective learning exercise*

Act of connection - say what?

This activity can be used to develop and discuss listening skills in teachers and in students. The activity below is as used with students.

- Students need to be in pairs, as well separated from other pairs as is possible. One student is A, the other is B.

- A has to talk to B for one minute on a subject of their choice, while B demonstrably does not listen.

- Then B does the same to A.

(Continued)

(Continued)

- Then A talks to B for one minute on a subject of their choice, while B listens carefully and shows they are doing so.
- Then B does the same to A.

Note: the first part of this often ends in uproarious laughter!

- Then in pairs, discuss how you know when someone is listening/not listening, and what relevance that has to them as students, and to you as their teacher.

As always, try to make ongoing use of this type of activity, rather than as a one off. Points to follow up for students and teachers will always arise, so you need to make sure that you as teacher and your students take responsibility for any decisions taken and follow them through.

Questioning

Questioning can help to clarify matters and help people to think more carefully about what they have said and done. It can also help them move forward from that and find ways out of difficult situations or find solutions to difficult problems. The skilled helper can use questioning, combined with active listening, in a range of situations and circumstances, such as to identify positives where learning has taken place but students have not recognised this, and to help clear up misconceptions.

 *Reflective learning exercise*

Act of connection – question time

- Give your students a topic to be a focus for questioning. This could involve big topics such as 'technology in the modern world' or 'world poverty', or smaller or more local topics such as 'last week's reading' or 'the college', or any topic which is part of the course of study.
- Split the students into groups, each with flipchart paper and pens.
- Students generate questions relating to the topic within a set time limit (five or ten minutes), and put them on the flipchart.
- No answers or opinions are allowed, just questions about the topic from different angles.
- Share and discuss the results, and use them to build some answers and/or courses of action.
- Ensure all students get copies of the results.

These two acts of connection can start to build trust from teacher to student, student to student and student to teacher, and using them is part of using helping skills. In addition, topics which are relevant for the subject being taught are being covered, but in a highly student-centred manner.

Pedagogic feature

Brandes and Ginnis – classroom management strategies for student-centred learning

Brandes and Ginnis have one particularly useful section in their 1996 book where they summarise 14 'basic management strategies which can form the foundation of a student-centred classroom' (Brandes and Ginnis, 1996: 32). I believe all teachers will find something useful in these strategies, so have included an adapted version of those strategies here. All of these strategies have principles for building trust embedded within them.

1 The circle – spend at least some time with your group sitting in a circle (a circle which includes you). See the act of connection following this section for more on this strategy.

2 The round – provide opportunities for each person in the circle to make a contribution, and for all to have done so before anyone comments on any of the contributions. Students are allowed to 'pass' if they do not wish to comment. This provides an opportunity to contribute in an atmosphere where all contributions are valued.

3 Listening skills – the use of active listening as already described earlier in this chapter.

4 Wordstorming (called 'brainstorming' in 1996, and long since changed) – the students are asked to come up with as many ideas as they can in a short time, and the person asking (teacher or student) writes them down as fast as they can until the pace of words being generated slows. This is a really good way of generating lots of ideas quickly.

5 The waiting game – when you want to gain the attention of your group, just sit quietly until everyone in the room also does so. You do need to have agreed this as a strategy with your students first, and it means that they are taking responsibility for paying attention.

6 Ground rules – work with the students to produce an agreed set of ground rules for your sessions, which all members of the group agree on. The intention is that students and teachers are more likely to stick to ground rules and self-manage their own group dynamic if they have agreed the ground rules themselves.

7 Sabotage – firstly ask students to share their thoughts on how they could sabotage the learning in your sessions if they wanted to, and discuss why, when and how this could happen. When students are disruptive or uncooperative, you can then ask the group who they think is involved in some sabotage at that time, and this can lead to self-management of disruption by the students and reduce the chances of sabotage over a period of time.

8 Assertiveness – use of the well-known 'broken record' technique with your students (although, of course, modern technology has rendered the term 'broken record' somewhat redundant) where you:

o state your point of view or request

o actively listen to the other person's point of view

o calmly restate your own

o actively listen as before

o continue as with a 'broken record' with repetition of the idea and process.

(Continued)

(Continued)

When you need to positively assert an idea or point in discussion or conversation but do not wish to lessen the value of a different perspective, this strategy can work well. Students can also use it to build confidence.

9 Games – there are many educational and other topics which can be enlivened by games, and they can also help build group cohesion at an early stage of working with a group. A game can address a theme from a different perspective; offer a ready-made opportunity for student participation; provide a burst of fun and energy to enliven your session; and can be another way of rapidly drawing together ideas, thoughts and understandings from a range of perspectives.

10 Open discussion – the word 'open' is crucial here, as the key point of this type of discussion is that it is student managed: that is the students decide and agree on the topic, prepare and carry out the discussion, and manage it themselves without any teacher intervention. Open discussions can sometimes be slow to get started, but can draw in those who often are too shy to contribute, and draw out what students really think, know or understand about a topic or theme.

11 Affective learning skills – this is about recognising the presence of emotion in and beyond the teaching context, acknowledging your and your students' attitudes and values towards the subject and other things, and allowing for these affective areas in your sessions. It does require the teacher, and indeed the students, to develop their helping skills, but it can result in a safe space for students to speak freely and receive support from each other and from the teacher in a way which powerfully builds trust.

12 Telling the truth – this is about realness and being yourself with your students, and in essence about honestly explaining why and how the teaching and learning works, and how they can get the best from it, including when you believe it will be more challenging and difficult.

13 Ask them – this is about asking your students, and features in one of the following acts of connection.

14 Valuing mistakes – mistakes always happen, and even teachers make them sometimes! This needs to be acknowledged, but also needs to be discussed and reflected on with and by your students, so that we can all learn from our mistakes, and be helped not to make them the next time.

These types of strategies and approaches can contribute significantly to developing trust and the more positive self-concept and motivation of students from the start of your interactions with them. They are all located within the practical connection of the connected professional, but are also relevant to the democratic and civic connection in their intention to develop a democratic learning community.

 *Reflective learning exercise*

Act of connection – learning circles

Every now and again, depending on how often you see your students, ask everyone present to sit in a circle. The aim is for everyone to feel this is a safe place where people can express opinions and speak freely, with no right or wrong answers, and where everyone will let everyone else speak.

Contributions are encouraged but voluntary and all those in the circle (including the teacher) respect what everyone else says.

The advantages include:

- everyone can see each other, hear each other and make eye contact
- speaking to each other becomes easy
- listening to each other actively is more possible
- the teacher is visibly a member of the group
- all are equal with no barriers
- a group feeling develops
- non-attentive behaviour becomes difficult.

The disadvantages include:

- students may feel exposed and shy at first
- the way the learning space is configured may make rearranging the furniture difficult.

Act of connection – ask them

You should not make all the decisions about learning if you are a people-centred teacher. Some decisions should belong to the students, so ask them questions such as:

- How can we all manage this assessment?
- Who will tell us about the progress they are making?
- What parts of it are worrying you?
- What can we do to help with this problem?
- How can we help those who are not feeling safe enough to participate?

In order to help this strategy succeed, you need firstly to show your students that you do listen to and act on their ideas when they come up with their own answers, and that the trust in the group is strong enough to make asking them work. Once they recognise that you do value and take note of their opinions and ideas, students normally begin to take more responsibility for themselves and their learning.

What evidence is there that building trust works?

The Education Endowment Foundation (EEF)

Chapter 2 provided examples of some of the thinking used in people-centred teaching, how the ideas have been used in practice and how their benefits have been evaluated. There are two particularly good sources to reference when you are looking for evidence about different teaching approaches, strategies and methods. One is the Education Endowment Foundation (EEF), which is one of the best known educational organisations evaluating education and how it works. The EEF evaluates evidence of learning gains, publishes these evaluations, and funds research to find out and test what does work in teaching, and what does not. There is much talk about 'evidence-based practice' in education, and much worry about reducing education to a set of toolbox principles, but the EEF takes a rigorous and thorough approach to its work, and is an excellent place to access evaluations about a wide range of aspects of school education. The EEF, as with many other large educational organisations, has largely neglected FE up until now, but it funded its first research into 'post-16 education' in March 2017, and this will hopefully increase its reach into FE.

The EEF aims 'to raise the attainment of 3–18 year olds, particularly those facing disadvantage; develop their essential life skills; and prepare young people for the world of work and further study' (EEF, 2017a). There is not as strong a human focus as would be hoped, and too strong a priority on education for work perhaps, but it is useful nevertheless. The EEF evaluates evidence from studies in particular themes and draw conclusions based on the cost of the intervention, the strength of the research evidence, and the impact shown from the evidence on student achievement. The EEF has a particularly interesting strand of work called their 'Teaching and Learning Toolkit' which is described as 'an accessible summary of the international evidence on the teaching of 5–16 year olds' (EEF, 2017b).

Evidence-based teaching (Petty, 2006)

The other source of evidence about different teaching approaches is Geoff Petty's book '*Evidence-Based Teaching*' (2006). The research used, again, mainly refers to schools, but I agree with Petty in arguing that the evidence is strongly relevant to FE. Even back in 2006, when this book was published (another edition was published in 2009), Petty was arguing that research into education had created 'an avalanche of information on what works and why' (Petty, 2006: ix). The book successfully marshals evidence relating to 'the strategies that are known to have the greatest average effect on student achievement, and to understand why these efforts work' (2006: 5). The more hard line approaches to evidence-based teaching have a lot to answer for, but Petty's version as laid out below is one I would recommend to people-centred teachers.

Evidence-based teaching does not dictate what you should do: it just shows you how best to achieve your own values, priorities and goals. You will still need to provide the creativity and judgement needed to decide on the best methods, and how to apply them in the context of your own teaching (2006: 5).

 Spotlight on pedagogy

Examples of people-centred teaching at work

The three examples of research reviews from the EEF Teaching and Learning Toolkit which follow have been selected because they are evaluations of approaches which are directly aligned to people-centred teaching. The EEF appoints teams of researchers to evaluate particular strategies and interventions, and reviews a significant amount of available research evidence, which are then evaluated against their cost, the security of the evidence and their impact on learner achievement. The selected examples all demonstrate a good balance between cost, evidence and impact. The examples are collaborative learning, peer tutoring, and social and emotional learning (SEL).

Collaborative learning

EEF (2017c: 1) defines collaborative learning as 'learning tasks or activities where students work together in a group small enough for everyone to participate on a collective task that has been clearly assigned. This can be either a joint task where group members do different aspects of the task but contribute to a common overall outcome, or a shared task where group members work together throughout the activity.' The achievement gain in studies reviewed by the EEF is 'moderate', the cost 'very low' and the evidence 'extensive'. In EEF terms, this is a good example of what works. Collaborative learning though 'requires much more than just sitting pupils together and asking them to work together; structured approaches with well-designed tasks' and 'approaches which promote talk and interaction between learners' also lead to the best learning gains (EEF, 2017c: 1).

Peer tutoring

EEF (2017d: 1) defines peer tutoring as 'a range of approaches in which learners work in pairs or small groups to provide each other with explicit teaching support ... The common characteristic is that learners take on responsibility for aspects of teaching and for evaluating their success.' The achievement gain in studies reviewed by the EEF is 'moderate', the cost 'very low' and the evidence 'extensive'. In EEF terms, this is another good example of what works.

Social and emotional learning (SEL)

EEF (2017e: 1) defines social and emotional learning as seeking to improve 'the social and emotional dimensions of learning, as opposed to focusing directly on the academic or cognitive elements of learning. SEL interventions might focus on the ways in which students work with (and alongside) their peers, teachers, family or community.' The achievement gain in studies reviewed by the EEF is 'moderate', the cost 'moderate' and the evidence 'extensive'. In EEF terms, this is another good example of what works. It can also clearly be seen to align well with people-centred teaching, and particularly with the work of Katherine Weare which has already been introduced in Chapter 2.

 Reflective learning exercise

Act of connection - using research evidence in your teaching

- Think of a small improvement you feel you could make in your own teaching which might improve the confidence, capabilities and achievement of your students.
- Take a look at the EEF's website and find one topic from their 'Teaching and Learning Toolkit' (https://educationendowmentfoundation.org.uk/resources/teaching-learning-toolkit) which could help you to create your own small 'act of connection'.
- By way of example, we'll use 'collaborative learning'. One of the courses you teach already has an assessed group presentation activity which you have wanted to update and refresh.

(Continued)

(Continued)

- Carefully browse the evidence and examples on the EEF website and use them to help you in your redesign.

- Put the first version forward to your students and seek their opinions. Finalise the changed assessment activity, and include in the next run of the course. Evaluate once results are in to include feedback from students and yourself, analysis of the results and comparisons with last year's results.

- Share the results with at least one other colleague.

Learning gains should have taken place, and you will have just experimented with people-centred teaching.

Building trust with colleagues

Working with colleagues when it works well, has been described as 'a supportive alliance for the quest' (Wadkins et al., 2004: 77), and is itself a process of building trust and mutual respect, only it is taking place between teachers rather than students. Although teachers in FE rarely now team teach (that is more than one teacher collaborating to teach together – at the same time – on a single course), they are often part of a subject team or team for a particular qualification or cross-institutional function such as learning support or English and Mathematics.

Working in direct collaboration with colleagues does have its own particular advantages and disadvantages. The disadvantages include:

- the challenges of maintaining effective communication across a team

- creating, storing and accessing of resources used across the team

- students experiencing a mixture of weaknesses across a teaching team

- inconsistency of teaching approach and topic coverage and even, at times, teachers actively disagreeing about approach and content through their teaching.

The advantages include:

- a wider variety of teaching styles and viewpoints for the students to experience

- a richer learning experience for the students

- a mixture of experience and strengths across a team

- pooling of teacher expertise

- sharing of aspects of teaching responsibility and administration

- well moderated and more consistent teaching, assessment and achievement.

Although there is not as much research to support the value of collaborative teaching as there is for collaborative learning, it is reasonable, based on the evidence, to expect good quality collaboration to help teachers improve individually and across teams (as we will consider further in Chapter 6), and for good quality collaboration to improve student achievement. Overall, as Wadkins et al. (2004: 93) suggest, we work collaboratively with other teachers because we 'enjoy the shared expertise, the interplay of teaching with another, having an alliance in the teaching experience, as well as the flexibility involved in sharing the duties.' But the strongest reason is perhaps because we 'enjoy the professional growth that occurs' and that we become the 'teacher as learner' (2004: 93).

Act of connection - lets work together

Work with at least one other colleague:

- swap lesson plans for similar or the same teaching sessions
- identify the things you have, could or might use from the other person's plans and why
- consider one or two items you would not use and why
- produce another lesson plan together
- agree to visit and peer observe in the near future, and work together soon on another item.

Building leadership trust

Among the many leadership approaches which have been researched, advocated, demonstrated and debated, one which has particular relevance to people-centred teaching is 'relational leadership'. This is not an entirely new idea, and is based on the notion that leadership is not just about individual leaders, but about a process which all are involved in. Relational leadership is about creating positive relationships and interactions within an organisation. Stephens and Carmeli (2015), in their study of relational leadership and creativity, argue that good workplace learning, creativity and productivity are fostered through 'mutually co-constructed interactions, rather than through the top-down influences' of leaders. They suggest that the positive, trusting and collaborative approaches used and fostered by relational leaders through 'respectful engagement' and 'readiness to learn' across all levels of the organisation are what motivate teams and individuals (Stephens and Carmeli, 2015: 6-7).

Stephens and Carmeli also found evidence that the respectful engagement involved fostered a greater sense of meaning for workers and greater motivation through greater autonomy. They conclude that, at its best, relational leadership results in 'mutual empowerment and growth' (2015: 27). Essentially this is applying the same thinking as we are proposing is used with students to get the best results, but applying it to FE organisations. Treat the staff as if you value, respect and listen to them, and they are much more likely to work well than if you don't.

Reflective learning exercise

Act of connection – one thing leads to another

By now you are probably thinking 'this sounds great, but how does it fit into the harsh environment of FE?' The answer is probably not at the top of your organisation. Where it can (and indeed does) fit, is within and across the subject team, learning support team, other cross organisational teams and administration teams. If and when you get the chance to lead a team remember the following advice. Remember Egan's helping skills? Why not use them with each other?

- In a staff or team meeting, or an informal get together of your team, propose an 'active listening' session. (Don't forget you have to listen actively too!)
- Each person in turn has two minutes to explain 'one thing they would like to change in the team'.
- The other participants listen carefully then ask clarifying questions.
- The group then has a general discussion to consider accepting the change, and it is then added either to the list of 'accepted changes', or list of 'changes not accepted'.
- All then discuss and agree what to do with the agreed change.
- The next meeting reviews changes accepted to see how they have worked.
- The not accepted list is reviewed periodically to see if any items should be moved to the list of accepted changes.

Golden moments and troubled times

Lunenberg et al. (2007) use the term 'golden moments' to describe incidents within the day-to-day work of education which can help to demonstrate just what can be achieved from excellent teaching. This can happen in any teaching session and can be a golden moment from the teacher or the student. It is important to recognise and, if possible capture, those moments, as they can help teachers and students to reflect more deeply on their own teaching and learn from that reflection. There is some debate about the value of emphasising and capturing golden moments. Research from Freedman et al. (2005) finds evidence that this sharing and reflecting on moments to support reflection is not always productive, and that it also does not necessarily always lead to action from the teachers or students which will enhance or transform their practice or learning. Reale (2009) on the other hand, emphasises that modelling through golden moments is a two-way process where all learn from each other, and found a range of benefits with shared expertise and understanding between students and other students, students and teachers, and teachers and other teachers.

Overall I believe that highlighting golden moments, particularly student golden moments, is a good thing, but you do need to be aware of the sensitivities of those who perhaps do not have golden moments as often as others.

Act of connection – golden moments

- Propose early in your course as part of the ground rules, that you will promote the idea of sharing golden moments during the year, and agree what this may mean (i.e. personal golden moments; learning golden moments; family golden moments etc.).

- Regularly ask your students for their golden moment/s of the week (ensure all students over a period of time do have opportunities to talk about their golden moments), and keep an informal record (perhaps on a cumulative PowerPoint) of the results.

- Towards the end of the year, review them all and celebrate what they meant then and what they now mean.

Troubled times

Just as often as we may have 'golden moments' (or even more often sometimes) there are also 'troubled times', when someone, something or some group just didn't quite work out as all had hoped or intended. You've prepared your session well, using activities which have worked well before, but it just doesn't work. Your students are just about to get their results for their last assessment, and their minds are clearly not on the class; one student in particular is grumpy, uncooperative but not quite disruptive. These are all examples of 'troubled times' and of course there can be much more severe troubles than the ones mentioned here, including major disruption and even violence. I have found very little research on this area, but what little there is seems to agree that this can happen at times. Teaching and learning are not exact sciences, and one person's golden moment may even be another person's troubled time. The advice generally is to reflect carefully on the troubled time in the same way as a golden moment, and to include the students in that reflection, and for all concerned to learn from it. When it happens, you may have enough confidence in your capacity to adapt your teaching to change the session and perhaps even convert it to a 'golden moment'. Even Ofsted do not expect outstanding teachers to be outstanding all the time, and no one could be. When I have been a student myself I have also experienced troubled times, but have not let them stop me learning.

Act of connection – troubled time

- Ask your student for their own examples of troubled times (be prepared to share your own).
- Why do they think they happened?
- What effect did they have?

(Continued)

> *(Continued)*
>
> - How could they have been different?
> - How much difference do they make?
> - How can they be avoided or positively managed?
>
> Overall, with luck, you will have more golden moments than troubled times.

This chapter

This chapter has taken us further into one of the key building blocks of people-centred teaching with a detailed consideration of building trust. A series of strategies and techniques, from thinkers including Gerard Egan and Brandes and Ginnis, which teachers can use were introduced and explained, and acts of connection are provided for you to make use of in your own teaching. There is good evidence that these strategies and teaching interventions do help to build student confidence, motivation, creativity and trust and impact on student achievement, and some of this evidence was explored in this chapter. Building trust through teacher collaboration and relational leadership are suggested strategies and ideas which teachers and their leaders could make positive use of, and the chapter closed by considering the value of golden moments in teaching and learning, and how to positively manage troubled times.

Notes on further reading

Brandes, D. and Ginnis, P. (1996) *A guide to student-centred learning*. Leicester: Nelson Thornes.

Another classic teaching text you should be able to access either online or via a second hand purchase. It should release your inner progressive teacher, and contains many ideas, activities and strategies which still very much have their place in the current version of FE.

Education Endowment Foundation (2017b) 'Teaching and Learning Toolkit'. [online] at https://education endowmentfoundation.org.uk/resources/teaching-learning-toolkit/ accessed 02/08/17

Despite the current almost complete absence of FE research, this organisation and website does have much content which is worth regularly returning to. Browse and compare what you think works with what they think works, and see their approach as a rigorous and highly professional way of developing and carrying out research, and evaluating its benefits and disadvantages.

Geoff Petty – his own website: http://geoffpetty.com

Geoff is one of the best known and respected names in FE, and his website provides some very useful downloads and resources which you will find useful. The message from Geoff on the home page is for teachers to 'enjoy experimenting with these methods but don't expect to use them perfectly straight away. Make sure you understand why they should work, and adapt your use of them until they begin to work well' (Petty, 2017).

National Standards which are addressed by this chapter are:

1. Reflect on what works best in your teaching and learning to meet the diverse needs of learners.

2. Evaluate and challenge your practice, values and beliefs.

4. Be creative and innovative in selecting and adapting strategies to help learners to learn.

6. Build positive and collaborative relationships with colleagues and learners.

8. Maintain and update your knowledge of educational research to develop evidence-based practice.

9. Apply theoretical understanding of effective practice in teaching, learning and assessment drawing on research and other evidence.

10. Evaluate your practice with others and assess its impact on learning.

11. Manage and promote positive learner behaviour.

13. Motivate and inspire learners to promote achievement and develop their skills to enable progression.

17. Enable learners to share responsibility for their own learning and assessment, setting goals that stretch and challenge.

20. Contribute to organisational development and quality improvement through collaboration with others.

Chapter 4

Just teach 2 – Be organised

 ——— *Key learning points in this chapter* ———

Getting your head organised

Getting your heart organised

Getting your teaching organised

Helping your students get organised

Starting to get your career organised

Layers of organisation

Being people-centred as a teacher is essential, but being people-centred is less likely to succeed if you are not also organised. There are many layers of organisation, from being able to get places (such as work) on time and with regularity, to remembering and meeting deadlines, keeping teaching resources prepared and up to date and keeping on top of emails. Much of your regular day-to-day teaching relies on organisation of your teaching space, the activities, materials and other resources you will use, and of course providing assistance to your students with their own organisation as individuals and groups.

Trust, empathy and well-being are not terms which at first stand out as part of what one would usually call being organised, but knowing yourself, managing your emotions and feelings and having the skills needed to be able to interact successfully with your students and colleagues are as practical as they are emotional. Organisation is a very important component of the self-discipline and sensitivity in the process of building learning relationships with your students, as are the ways in which you maintain your own positivity and contribute to the competence, confidence and well-being of your colleagues and of your organisation. Keeping your emotions balanced when in challenging and stressful situations and maintaining positive communication at the same time needs a solid base of organised capabilities, processes and practices.

The chapter takes us through managing these subtle and different layers of organisation purposefully, to maintain balance in your teaching and your other responsibilities (and of course your life away from work) and to help your work be enjoyable and effective. Organisation makes a major difference to your day-to-day activity, and if you can be confident with organisation it has a knock-on effect on everything else. This chapter provides a framework for moving through the different layers of organisation step by step. These steps are:

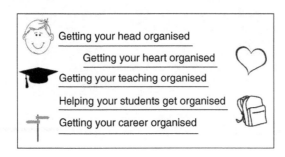

The chapter unashamedly mixes together some 'golden oldie' ideas and activities from the 1990s and the 2000s as well as from the last two or three years. Good ideas mature sometimes rather than merely grow old, and innovation is not only about being new and different! Let's get organised!

Getting your head organised

Personal planning by 'building your own rainbow'

There will be times in our personal and professional lives when we feel anxiety, a sense of dissatisfaction and a lack of a sense of direction. We are not sure why, but it can start to feel like 'we never really take charge of our own lives' (Hopson and Scally, 1999: 10). This is when we need to 'examine our lives from the outside and ourselves from the inside' (1999: 10). The argument is that our heads may tell us that we do not have control of what we are doing, and that our lives are controlled by others. There is of course some truth in that, but it is possible to take charge of our lives at least to some degree, and at best to achieve a significant degree of self-empowerment. If we believe that our learners have the capacity to self-actualise, surely we must also believe that we have that same capacity. Getting your head organised is an important part of your own personal self-actualisation, and what follows is a core activity which will help.

Reflective learning exercise

The idea of taking charge of our own lives to achieve self-empowerment sounds very sixties doesn't it, and to a degree it is, but Barrie Hopson and Mike Scally, who made use of these particular ideas over twenty years ago, and are still publishing books (among many other things) on 'life skills', and they have had much success promoting ideas and activities around what has been called a 'positive psychology' approach to life. They use the rainbow metaphor in a resource called 'Build your own rainbow', which was popular in education and business when published (most recently in 1999), to produce some excellent activities which really can help you to get your head organised (and, as we shall see, to get your heart organised too). The next section adapts one of Hopson and Scally's activities for people-centred teachers.

Act of connection – build your own rainbow

Firstly, sit back, close your eyes, and think of a rainbow. For many this is a symbol of 'hope, beauty and optimism' (Hopson and Scally, 1999: 11). The idea is not to find a pot of gold, but to hope to find your own true value, and to reflect on your own true value, and to use that in a positive way to review aspects of your life and work, and create optimistic and possible goals by 'building your own rainbows'. The techniques involved can be used with your students, your colleagues and your organisations with simple adaptations. Now answer these five basic questions, and their sub questions:

1 Who am I?

   i What are my own values, skills, understandings and interests?

   ii How am I spending my time?

   iii Do I know what I want to with my life and work and where I want to do it?

2 Where am I now?

   i What stage of my life am I at?

   ii What stage of my career am I at?

3 What am I satisfied with and what am I dissatisfied with?

   i What can an analysis of my life and work roles as adult, teacher, parent, friend, colleague and partner tell me?

4 What changes would I like to make?

   i How can I get better still at what I am already satisfied with?

   ii What small steps can I take towards changes I want to make?

5 How do I make changes happen?

   i How can I imagine and plan to make those changes happen?

You can break this activity down into several stages, and adapt it to specific tasks and activities, but it does give a comprehensive set of starting points in personal planning. I would suggest that you try to think of 'acts of connection' (something small and achievable to ensure initial success) which you or your students can undertake to achieve the changes and goals which have just been conceived.

Spotlight on pedagogy

Become a rainbow builder

Hopson and Scally (1999) suggest that we all need certain skills to become a rainbow builder? There are six.

- Knowing yourself – The ability to find time to reflect on your life and your work.

- Learning from experience – Using that time to reflect on incidents, activities, events and engagements, and consider what took place, what you learned from it, and how that can fit with your existing learning and expertise.

- Researching the social world you are part of – Finding out and learning more about the world you live and work in; finding out more about other people's worlds, including ideas and actions.

- Making decisions – Learning how to set focused goals or objectives and make plans without getting overwhelmed by too much information or too many needs and plans. Considering and choosing your actions from a range of alternatives depending on the circumstances of the time.

- Looking after yourself – Building rainbows is not easy. You need to 'look after yourself physically, rationally and emotionally' (Hopson and Scally, 1999: 14).

- Communicating – In order to make the most of the opportunities you identify, and to identify them in the first place, we all need to be able to 'express ourselves clearly, orally and on paper' (Hopson and Scally, 1999: 14).

The steps and the associated skills and capabilities can be mixed and approached in many ways, and not all of them are always needed. Whether they are used to review a teaching session, discuss student work such as presentations, contribute to a CPD event or even to help review evidence for Ofsted, making use of these rainbow building steps, approaches and questions can shed an optimistic but focused light which will really help you to get your head organised.

Getting your heart organised

Establishing and maintaining emotional well-being

As we have already seen in this book, there are many ways of describing our human ways of feeling and behaving, and how we can positively make use of them in teaching and learning. These have included Carl Rogers and the core conditions for a 'helping relationship', Katherine Weare and a 'learning relationship', and Vicky Duckworth (see p. 92) arguing for FE teaching professionals to care for each other and their well-being. This is of course not only a matter of the heart, but this next section focuses on 'emotional well-being' which is primarily about feelings and emotions which can be equally difficult at times as matters of the head, if not more so.

Emotional well-being

Stewart-Brown (2000: 32) defines emotional well-being as being present 'when a range of feelings, among them energy, confidence, openness, enjoyment, happiness, calm and caring are combined and balanced'. Dealing with emotions is not simple, but as we have seen so far, it is an essential part of education. To act and teach in ways which promote emotional well-being, according to Weare requires capability in 'self-understanding; understanding, expressing and managing our emotions, and understanding and making relations (2004: 23).' If we can learn from developing these capabilities in ourselves we will be more able to support our students' own emotional well-being.

There are two key arguments as to why we should address well-being. First, looking after the well-being of teachers and their students is morally just and ethically appropriate for a profession which has such a long-term impact on people's lives. Secondly, research shows (as we have seen in Chapter 3) that it does make a difference, and improves motivation, learning, student achievement and fulfilment. Warwick et al. (2006) carried out an FE-based 'scoping study' which drew on a literature review; interviews with key people in 13 organisations with an interest in promoting student mental health in this sector; a postal survey of 150 FE colleges in England and case studies of five colleges with experience of addressing mental health issues among younger students. This small but important study located evidence of processes and practices which were likely to enhance student emotional well-being, and potentially attainment, including greater awareness among staff at all levels of students' issues with mental health; a positive whole organisation well-being focused ethos and approach; and support for individual students including counselling and opportunities for students to make their views known. The research also found causes for concern, including limited linkages between FE organisations and mental-health-related external organisations; few suitable trained staff; pressure on resources to provide services and disseminate good practice; and a limited amount of evidence of the direct impact of the efforts to improve emotional well-being.

A review of school-based interventions for promoting well-being argued more confidently that evidence 'shows that interventions which take this multi-level, comprehensive "whole organisation" or "whole system" approach are more likely to have a positive impact in relation to outcomes' (Anna Freud Research Centre and Public Health England, 2016: 7). School-based studies by Domitrovich et al. (2010) and Langford et al. (2014) are cited by this publication and both consider the impact of approaches to promoting student health and well-being, and find good evidence that there is a positive impact on achievement.

Developing and promoting emotional well-being – factors to consider

Bear this advice in mind when engaging in any activities promoting well-being or any other potentially sensitive feelings, emotions or situations. The previously cited Anna Freud Research Centre and

(Continued)

(Continued)

Public Health England (2016) study reminds all those involved of essential factors to consider when working with well-being. These are:

- Ensuring that students and/or staff know what this is for 'who will see it, and what difference it will make' (2016: 37)

- Taking part in well-being related activities can have emotional impact on participants

- It may be necessary for some parts of activities to be completed privately

- Some students may need support to help them participate openly and honestly

- Introducing the activity clearly and well is crucial.

 *Reflective learning exercise*

Act of connection – positive postcards

Working with trusted others who will join you in discussing your responses with some sensitivity (i.e. friends, colleagues or family) would be very helpful when working on this activity.

- Draw a diagram, mind map, cartoon or any other visual representation of what you believe are your main personal qualities and characteristics. This represents who you are right now.

- Choose at least three things you like about yourself and write them on a postcard or sticky note (or on a tablet, smartphone or laptop).

- Write three things you like about someone else (preferably someone you can share this with!).

- Consider why you like your three things and those of someone else.

- Share your cards with at least two other people and, if possible, display all the cards and comments together and discuss these questions:

What could you do to turn the 'new likes' into reality?

How has this activity made you feel?

This activity provides a very small starting point exemplifying the positive and growth-focused approach to emotional well-being which is part of people-centred teaching. Follow-up activities could be to turn the results of this activity into an action plan, or to use it to update a previous plan. The use of this type of activity helps us to organise the heart to support our people-centred teaching. The skills and understanding concerned are within the practical connection of the connected professional, but can be used in all the other three connections.

Getting your teaching organised

Curriculum planning - constructive alignment

There is one approach to organising teaching which has always made sense to me and most teachers I know, and it is also clear and straightforward to understand. 'Constructive alignment' (Biggs, 2003) starts with the question 'what do we want our students to achieve (i.e. be able to do, understand and apply) as a result of their learning?'

As the name suggests, the idea is that all the different aspects and components of your learning programme line up together or are in alignment, so that they can combine to help our students do, understand and apply the learning they have signed up for. This involves aims, learning outcomes or objectives, approaches, methods, assessment and evaluation and also the process of learning which is most likely to assist in the alignment of the whole curriculum. External or organisational influences or drivers, such as qualification requirements, need to be included but be careful not to include too many elements in your curriculum planning as it can become increasingly difficult to align. There is evidence that constructive alignment can help students develop deeper learning approaches (Wang et al., 2013) and engagement and achievement (Reaburn et al., 2009), and regularly asking the question below of every part of your curriculum can be really useful:

> Are my aims, objectives, methods, assessments, evaluation and any external expectations all aligned towards achieving the intended student learning?

If the answer is yes, this is encouraging; but if the answer is no, this can prove to be a straightforward way of starting to identify what may need to come into further alignment.

ASSUREd planning

A very practical way of ensuring constructive alignment and helping to get your teaching organised, is the ASSURE model of planning. This fits into the philosophy of people-centred teaching as it is based on Gagne's (1985) idea that learning is influenced by the 'internal conditions' of the students such as their experiences and capabilities and the 'external conditions' of the students, including among other things, the teacher, the organisation and the curriculum requirements. In order to plan for achievement in a way which acknowledges this, the ASSURE model proceeds on the basis that people

(Continued)

(Continued)

learn more effectively when the teaching helps them to learn for themselves, rather than when it is intended to fill them up from empty vessels. There are six steps in the ASSURE model, and they are:

1. Analyse your students

Step 1 is about finding out more about your students, their needs and their characteristics. This includes age, ethnicity, gender, entry level, existing skills, attitudes, circumstances and needs, learning styles and preferences (useful but do not over use them). Some of this you will know from information that you are provided, and some of it you will need to find out.

2. State objectives

Writing objectives or learning outcomes is essential in order to have a clear indication of what students should learn in your sessions, but I personally believe that well-written objectives do not necessarily always result in good teaching. To have a clear idea of what you want your students to learn, and how they will feel about that is essential, and objectives will help that.

3. Select methods and resources

Once you have stated your objectives, selecting the right methods and resources to achieve those objectives is equally important. There will be several combinations of methods and resources which will work, so you can tailor these to the group, or situation, or course you are planning for.

4. Utilise methods and resources

Once you have decided on your methods and resources you need to decide how, when and where to use them.

5. Require student participation

'Require' sounds somewhat harsh, but it is well recognised that people learn through experience and activity, and that participation in the learning process is the main way for this to happen. Creating an atmosphere which encourages participation, and organising activities which give it the best chance of taking place is more difficult to control than passive learning, but it is much more fruitful.

6. Evaluate and revise

This can fall off the end of a session quite easily when there are time and content pressures, but it is really important that there are regular opportunities in your teaching sessions to think about what learning actually did take place and how that worked for your students and yourself. Some quick evaluative activities such as the 'three word wonder' can be very helpful.

Act of connection – three word wonder

- Ask all your students to write three words which they think summed up the session for them on sticky notes.
- Collect the sticky notes and put them on display.
- Ask everyone to read and comment on them.
- Make a copy of them all to share with the group

Curriculum planning strategies such as constructive alignment and the ASSURE approach are firmly within the practical connection of the connected professional, but also underpin the other three connections.

Helping your students get organised

Students are in many ways just like their teachers. Some are really organised as individuals and in groups, some are not at all organised and some are fairly organised. If they are to contribute to their own learning, identify and achieve their own goals, become more capable human beings and make the world a better place, being able to work together with others and be organised is going to be needed.

Tuckman and group development

One of the best-known approaches to understanding how people can and do work together and the dynamics of what can make this successful comes from Bruce Tuckman. He created his 'forming, storming, norming and performing' model of group development back in 1965 (I was just 14 years old). Bonebright (2010) carried out a review of the uses of Tuckman 40 years after the model had been introduced. It was found to be one of the most used and recognised models for developing and understanding group dynamics, partly because it is genuinely possible to apply it in a very wide range of situations, including education.

Tuckman's model has four stages which are:

1. Forming

The first stage is when a group orient themselves to their task or tasks, create ground rules and start testing boundaries with their behaviour and interpersonal engagement. Relationships inside and outside the group also begin to become established.

(Continued)

(Continued)

2. Storming

This stage is when conflict starts to emerge and this disrupts unity and collaboration. Group members withdraw as individuals and the group overall can show resistance to their task or tasks.

3. Norming

The group starts to develop cohesion in this third stage. Acceptance of other individuals and a consensus arrives about group norms and behaviours. The group is becoming a harmonious entity during this stage.

4. Performing

In this final stage, the group is able to adapt to achieve advanced problem solving and flexibility, cohesion and group energy is apparent.

Some of the evidence Tuckman used for the development of this model was over focused on therapeutic situations, and Tuckman himself agreed that this was the case. There was also little consideration of how groups change over time, and how circumstances outside of the group itself could influence the development and success of a group (Bonebright, 2010). This has not affected the degree to which the model has been used, and in my teaching experience I have found that it does provide some helpful ideas and explanations of what is happening when groups work well and not so well, and a really useful way of helping me as a teacher understand groups, and help them to work better, both as individuals and as groups.

 Reflective learning exercise

Act of connection – using Tuckman

- Using one group which you teach, and a hard copy of Tuckman's group stages, consider how the development of that group reflects Tuckman's stages of development, and if or how it moved through the different stages.
- How much did you influence how that group functioned?
- Did they arrive at the performing stage?
- What could have been done differently?

Broaden your thinking to your own team in the workplace and your organisation.

- Where do you think they currently are in Tuckman's stages? How may they reach or sustain the 'performing' stage?

Starting to get your career organised

As has already been made clear in this book, the FE sector is complex, under pressure and constantly changing. This can make teaching in the sector a career which may not seem as desirable as others. We have also, however, seen the potential to make a difference which exists in FE, and the capacity to engage with diverse students and a range of teaching styles and subjects. A study of over 3,000 staff in FE found that over 85 per cent felt they were making a contribution to society (Villeneuve-Smith et al., 2008). However, over 90 per cent in the same study also regularly worked more than their contracted hours. This is a typical snapshot of working in the FE sector.

 *Spotlight on pedagogy*

An identity to strive for

We have already outlined characteristics of people-centred teaching in FE, professional values, and a number of aspects of what can genuinely be called an aspirational identify for teachers in FE. Gregson at al. (2015) articulately argue that there is a positive professional identity which FE teachers can aspire to and work for. Their vision of this identity argues that professional FE teachers should be able to:

- achieve 'satisfaction, commitment, well-being and effectiveness' (2015: 14)

- achieve a 'healthy balance between personal, work and external policy challenges' (2015: 14)

- draw 'coherence from their underlying values and beliefs' (2015: 14).

- affect their learners in 'positive, educational and life-enhancing ways' (2015: 14).

This directly reinforces the central concept of this book, which is that people-centred teachers are people-centred people.

Establishing your professional identity

Early in your career there are a number of key actions you can take which will put you on the road to establishing that strong professional identity and which will help to sustain teaching as a career, and take you forward towards being a connected professional (with thanks to Gregson et al., 2015).

- Learn how to support, develop and manage yourself.

- Make and take opportunities to work with other colleagues inside your team and outside.

- Get involved in some sort of development activity or research which can build your academic and professional scholarly competence.

- Learn to be patient, resilient, reflective and indefatigable.

- Be prepared to stand up for your values and your profession.

(Continued)

> (Continued)
>
> The final action does require confidence and courage, but FE teachers are a group of professionals who need a voice now at least as much as they ever have done. Hafez uses metaphors from dance and fairy tales when emphasising the importance of the need to assert a professional identity and to use that voice, before it is too late. 'We can break down the door and tell the king in no uncertain terms not just that we will dance but that we are the composers and the choreographers of the music and the dance' (2015: 162).

This chapter

This chapter has moved through several important stages in your development as a people-centred teacher, starting with matters of the head, and developing the self-awareness and self-confidence you need to do this work, and moving on to matters of the heart, and the needs for emotional engagement and emotional well-being for teachers and students. Two ways of planning and preparing your curriculum and your teaching sessions (constructive alignment and ASSURE) were recommended, as well as some strategies from Tuckman which will assist you to understand and manage the group dynamics among your students, and support your students in organising themselves. The chapter closes with advice and suggestions about how you can develop your teaching and career in ways which will help you to claim and represent the positive autonomous characteristics of an FE teaching professional.

Notes for further reading

Biggs, J. (2003) *Aligning teaching for constructing learning.* York: Higher Education Academy.

This book, which you should easily find with a google search, is a straightforward and clear explanation of constructive alignment.

Bonebright, D.A. (2010) '40 years of storming: a historical review of Tuckman's model of small group development', *Human Resource Development International,* 13(1), pp.111–120.

If you are interested in the Tuckman model, this is a good journal article to find out more. Extracts from the article abstract give you a good idea about the content of the paper.

> This paper presents a historical overview of the Tuckman model describing the stages of group development . . . the model has a unique history in that it was initially popular among HRD [Human Resource Development] practitioners and later became common in academic literature as well. Its significance was a reflection of its time, responding both to the growing importance of groups in the workplace and to the lack of applicable research.
>
> (Bonebright, 2010: 111)

If you cannot get access to the journal article, try http://infed.org/mobi/bruce-w-tuckman-forming-storming-norming-and-performing-in-groups/ from the excellent infed.org website.

Warwick, I., Maxwell, C., Simon, A., Statham, J. and Aggleton, P. (2006) *Mental health and emotional well-being of students in further education – a scoping study*. London: Thomas Coram Research Unit Institute of Education.

You should be able to locate an electronic copy of this document from a google search or a search on Google scholar. Mental health and emotional well-being are very much current concerns in FE, and although this piece of research was now published 11 years ago, and the work it reports on took place in 2005 and 2006, it is still well worth reading. The conclusions of the research indicated that student mental health was a growing problem, and made some helpful recommendations including 'better use of existing policies and guidance, continuing professional development, closer partnership working between colleges and local CAMHS, and making resources available to disseminate existing good practice' (Warwick et al., 2006: 4).

National Standards which are addressed by this chapter are:

1. Reflect on what works best in your teaching and learning to meet the diverse needs of learners.

4. Be creative and innovative in selecting and adapting strategies to help learners to learn.

9. Apply theoretical understanding of effective practice in teaching, learning and assessment drawing on research and other evidence.

10. Evaluate your practice with others and assess its impact on learning.

11. Manage and promote positive learner behaviour.

14. Plan and deliver effective learning programmes for diverse groups or individuals in a safe and inclusive environment.

17. Enable learners to share responsibility for their own learning and assessment, setting goals that stretch and challenge.

Chapter 5

Just teach 3 – Be connected

 Key learning points in this chapter

Navigating the digital swamp

What does work with digital technology?

Managing information overload

Network learning

Connecting communities

Technology for all manifesto

This chapter examines how digital technology can be used to support teaching and learning and how it can both draw students, teachers and communities together as well as keep them apart. In this chapter, the hyperbole often associated with digital technology is avoided, and clear, informed practical advice and guidance are all provided. The perspective guiding this chapter is rooted in the conviction that technology, when harnessed well by teachers, students, and communities at large, can and does make a real difference to their lives, and can assist with deep, people-centred learning. If, where and when it does not do that (which is regularly in education settings), using technology can be an expensive waste of time and energy, and other tools which support learning should be used instead.

Navigating the digital swamp

Introducing the digital swamp

When researching and writing this chapter, I was delighted to discover that Michael Fullan has written about the use of technology in education. His work on change management is accessible and makes sense to teachers, and the same is the case in this field. He takes a robust view of technology, and is prepared to forcefully critique its use when unsuccessful, which is not always the case. He starts a recent joint publication with the statement, 'the digital swamp is alive and growing - murky, uneven, helter-skelter, dangerous and exciting, with an ever-changing ecology' (Fullan and Donnelly, 2015: 1). He offers the ideas in this publication as a 'powerful tool to navigate your way through the swamp. But a fool with a tool is still a fool' (2015: 1). The reason for this tone then follows, with the statement 'we believe that it is accurate to say that the vast majority of the use of digital in schools around the world is either non-existent or superficial when it comes to learning' (2015: 1).

Fullan and Donnelly then cite one of the best-known experts in 'the digital' in suggesting that the main approach with the use of digital technologies is based on acquisition or to 'buy and keep on buying' (Laurillard, 2012). They provide a shocking example of the 'buy and keep on buying' approach where in the US, the Los Angeles school district (1,100 schools, 700,000 students and 46,000 teachers) purchased iPads and associated apps for $1.3 billion in June 2013, only to cancel the contract by August 2014. An evaluation of the programme (Margolin et al., 2014) found that only one out of every 245 classrooms was using the curriculum accessed via the use of the iPads and that 'superficial or non-use was the norm' (Fuller and Donnelly, 2015: 1). Fullan and Donnelly are scathing in their judgement, stating that this 'is not surprising. The focus needs to be on pedagogy and implementation into classrooms, not on fast-tracking to the future through high profile digital acquisition. The allure of the shiny objects in the swamp seems irresistible' (2015: 1-2). This is one very large example of how ideas and projects can be plucked from the digital swamp and we will all almost certainly have our own examples from experience. The worrying thing about digital technology is that judgements about potential learning benefits and value for money, which are central to so many decisions in so many areas, are not applied in the same way with acquisition and use of digital technologies.

Act of connection - have you experience of the digital swamp?

Just ask yourself these questions:

- What contribution have electronic whiteboards made to deep student learning?
- How engaging and visually interesting is your Virtual Learning Environment (VLE)?
- How many other resources could you buy with half the budget spent by your organisation on technology?

- How many 'new dawns' and 'technology transformations' have you experienced?
- Can you remember the two or three sector wide plans for educational technology before FELTAG (Further Education Learning Technology Action Group) and ETAG (the same, interestingly without the 'learning' or the 'FE' bits!?)?

 Spotlight on pedagogy

The 'push' and 'pull' of change

Don't get the impression from this approach that I am an anti-technology Luddite. In fact, I completely agree with Fullan and Donnelly's (2015: 2) statement that 'if used properly digital can be an amazing accelerator for deep learning.' At present, Fullan and Donnelly (2015) suggest we are in a situation where the 'push and pull of change' or the series of forces affecting the world of education have left us with a stalemate. One key 'push' factor forcing educational change is argued to be the increasing boredom of students with education as they get older, and of teachers as they encounter this boredom in their students.

In UK FE, although there is evidence that some students are more difficult to engage, the local and national push factors forcing change are more often those already critiqued in this book. They are managerial or directional interventions from organisations and/or governments (often with no real experience of how to make the best use of technology) which leave teachers without a clear professional identity or autonomy but with very large workloads. This pushes them and their students towards a greater number of tests and examinations, reminding us of Biesta's 'valuing what we measure, not measuring what we value' (2010: 13).

One of the key 'pull' factors, or those which can pull us towards digital technology is the 'allure of digital', often offered as a solution to many educational problems, which can result in very little gain in learning, while using large amounts of increasingly scarce resources.

 Spotlight on pedagogy

Critical forces around the digital swamp

Fullan and Donnelly (2015: 4) argue that there are 'three critical forces that must work together' to get us out of the digital swamp and they are:

Managing Technology - digital technology has only been present since the later twentieth century and has grown massively, to the point where 'the swamp is alive with digital products being generated at a feverish pace' (Fullan and Donnelly, 2015: 4). It has happened so fast and in such an unplanned way that it has outrun our capacity to make the best use of digital for learning. Ways

(Continued)

(Continued)

of managing the pace with which the latest products drive educational choices rather than educational choices driving product purchases must be found.

Pedagogy – new understandings of pedagogy, or the methods and practices of teaching, (for example Hattie, 2012) suggest that we should be using 'a learning partnership with and among students that deepens and accelerates how and what students learn' (Fullan and Donnelly, 2015). Understanding, developing and using pedagogy with technology in education must move further than it has done to date. There is now a sound research base about helpful uses of technology and how to make use of them, but this needs to move from being in the background to a point at which we start using technology in education to its best advantage.

Change knowledge – the third critical force is about what we need to know to be able to cope with and manage change effectively. Defining and taking charge of this is of course not easy, but establishing ways in which teaching professionals and their students can shape and reshape ideas by constant engagement in a process of trying and keeping good ideas and trying and discarding not so good ideas is what will make a difference.

Later in the chapter we shall move on to propose that 'network learning' is one way of balancing, connecting and applying these three critical forces of change.

Spotlight on pedagogy

What works with digital technology?

This next section of the chapter provides two examples of high quality research which have considered the impact of technology. One authoritative report was published by NESTA, which is a well-known and respected 'innovation foundation'. An expert panel was assembled for this report (Luckin et al., 2012) to review evidence from a very wide range of sources (starting with over 1,000 research studies and over 300 'teacher led interventions'), and found that 'students today inhabit a rich digital environment, but it is insufficiently utilised to support learning' (2012: 6), and that 'evidence of digital technologies producing real transformation in learning and teaching remains elusive' (2012: 8). They did however find evidence that the use of digital technologies could be seen to have real benefits for learning (bearing in mind that availability of suitable devices operating at a suitable speed need to be available for all for these benefits to happen). These benefits were not classified via different types of resources or subjects and topics, but rather by key aspects of learning.

Benefits for learning from digital technology

The benefits which were evidenced included:

- A *rich learning environment* which would otherwise not be available between experts and students can be created with high quality learning materials.

- Collaborative 'episodes of learning' with others facilitated by technology can stimulate self-awareness, understanding and confidence in students.
- 'Learning through making' (that is creating visible physical outputs from learning activity) can be extended into new areas.
- Learning through exploring has 'immense potential' (Luckin et al., 2012: 31).
- Technology-supported inquiry (that is helping students to undertake challenges and other activities in a problem-focused way) can also be enhanced.

The use of digital technology, then, has much potential, but has still not got near to fully realising that potential in education.

 Reflective learning exercise

Before considering what research suggests we should do to make the most of digital technology in education, here is a simple opportunity for you to reflect on your experiences of using digital technology.

Act of connection – staying out of the digital swamp

When you are considering using digital technology in a teaching session, or in any other way, treat it with the same considerations you would any other approach, technique or tool, and ask these questions *before* you use it.

- Has this been used before by me or others and did it result in deep learning?
- Is it easy to access and use?
- Is it strongly engaging?
- Is it available 24/7?
- Is it centred around real-life problem solving?
- How will I ensure it is evaluated by students and teachers?

 Spotlight on pedagogy

Escaping the digital swamp

Another significant evaluative report was carried out by the University of Durham for the Educational Endowment Foundation (Higgins et al., 2012). Initially, the evaluation encouragingly comments that 'the research evidence over the last forty years about the impact of digital technologies

(Continued)

(Continued)

on learning consistently identifies positive benefits' (2012: 3). Their investigations were not conclusive, and they find that a causal link between the use of digital technologies and achievement

> cannot be inferred from this kind of research. It seems probable that more effective schools and teachers are more likely to use digital technologies more effectively than other schools. We need to know more about where and how it is used to greatest effect, then investigate to see if this information can be used to help improve learning in other contexts. We do not know if it is the use of technology that is making the difference. (2012: 3)

They continue to argue that:

> it is not whether technology is used (or not) which makes the difference, but how well the technology is used to support teaching and learning. There is no doubt that technology engages and motivates young people. However this benefit is only an advantage for learning if the activity is effectively aligned with what is to be learned. It is therefore the pedagogy of the application of technology in the classroom which is important: the how rather than the what. This is the crucial lesson emerging from the research. (2012: 4)

The research outlines some helpful guidance for escaping the digital swamp as follows:

- be cautious in the face of technological solutions to educational challenges
- well organised collaborative uses of technology can be more effective than individual use
- technology tends to support short, focused interventions to improve learning rather than sustained use over a longer period
- using technology to help provide tutorial support for disadvantaged students and those with particular learning needs and/or disabilities can be helpful
- technology supplements regular teaching better than it replaces it
- properly resourced and sustained professional development for teachers in the use of digital technology which focuses on successful pedagogical uses is most successful in improving learning.

Managing information overload

One thing that we can all agree on is that we now have just about as much information at our fingertips as we have ever had, and a large proportion of that information can be accessed using digital technology. Team Radicati (2015) reported exponential growth in the use of email, forecasting that by 2019 there would be 2.9 billion worldwide users of email which is over one-third of the population of the world. They also report that the number of business emails sent and received per user per day is currently between 122 and 126, with over 90 received, or 450–500 received per five-day week. You may not quite get that many per day, but information overload is a real challenge to the working life of teachers today, given that there is also the further information contained in email attachments, awarding body regulations, teaching resources and quality management information and data to deal with, to name but a few. This book can't provide a way of completely stopping this, but here is a simple activity which should help you to better manage this digital overload.

Reflective learning exercise

Act of connection – 'do it, leave it, bin it and done it'

You have to be quite brave to take this on, but this activity can really help to prioritise what to do and when, or indeed if you actually need to do anything, and can reduce digital overload.

- Firstly this means you will need to say 'no' sometimes when others may expect you to say 'yes', so think carefully about it before you do so.
- Take your email inbox for example, and create four folders which can act as 'piles' of emails (do it on paper or with paper if that is better for you). These should be labelled 'do it', 'leave it', 'bin it' and 'done it' (the 'done it' folder should have the year on it, e.g. 'done it 2017/18').
- As the emails come in, quickly read them and put them in the appropriate folder.
- Do the 'do it' tasks first, then the 'leave tasks'. Leave the 'bin it' items alone for the moment. It's easy to monitor if this is working, as the 'do it' items should be constantly refreshed, and the 'done it' folder fills up.
- Check the 'bin it' folder perhaps once a week. If nothing has come back to haunt you, you can actually delete them, or of course move them into one of the other folders if that is needed.

This does take quite a bit of time initially, but you will soon see that it is saving you (and probably others) more time.

Spotlight on pedagogy

Network learning

Network learning was introduced in Chapter 1 and, as a reminder, it is a process which helps teaching professionals learn and teach together more effectively through the process of networking. This particular approach to networking emphasises the value of digital technology in the process of teacher and student learning, but as a facilitator of the process of networking, not necessarily the central component. How can you start to develop and join in network learning? Veugelers and O'Hair (2005) suggest that there are key elements in how network learning evolves, and I have adapted their ideas to provide some helpful guidelines for establishing FE-based network learning. All participants in a prospective network should:

- Work with a democratic and student-centred approach to teaching and learning.
- Encourage their teachers to reflect on and learn from their work and life experience.
- Provide a voice within and across networks for all participants.

(Continued)

(Continued)

- Use the network horizontally (that is through peer interaction and into the community beyond) to share a broad-based range of views, perspectives and experiences.

- Use the results to plan for, carry out and evaluate change.

- Provide ways in which participants can meet both virtually and face to face.

- Operate through shared ownership and inclusive leadership.

- Examine their own practices in terms of equality and diversity.

- Develop collaborative and connected actions.

- Be committed to accelerating change.

It will not be possible to make sure all of these elements are present at all times and stages of a network but try to include as many as possible if you are starting any network. Please don't forget – the use of technology reinforces and facilitates some of the community dimensions of the network, but does not dominate.

Network learning in action

The Education and Training Foundation has been funding a number of practitioner projects in FE aimed at 'empowering practitioners and teaching leadership staff to focus on effective practice that is most helpful for their own challenges' (ETF: 2017). These projects can provide good examples of network learning. One such example is the 'Clean Break' project, which involved collaboration between a London women's theatre company, five teachers from a local FE college and twenty female learners, 'with experience of the criminal justice system and women at risk of offending' (Sutter and McCluskey, 2016: 1). The project aimed to ensure all partners worked together to produce, use and evaluate new resources and approaches to developing the functional skills of the students. This was embedded within the context of performing arts and newly purchased laptops were utilised to provide opportunities for the participants to actively develop those skills. The project's final report found that there were clear benefits for students accruing from the collaboration of teachers and the active use of technology to provide in situ practising of functional skills; these combined well with the particularly student-focused approaches of the Clean Break staff. Growing personal confidence and a lower risk of offending or re-offending were both reported as project outputs and outcomes. Student feedback was particularly positive and this project locates well overall as an example of network learning, where people-centred teaching and technology work together well.

 Reflective learning exercise

Starting network learning

There is more about this type of activity in Chapter 6, but here is a simple starter. Ask these questions in a team meeting, or when chatting with your colleagues informally.

- If we were going to start a network what would we want it to be about and who would we want to join?
- What theme, topic or idea might we want to start with?
- How would we go about starting it?
- When shall we start?

Connecting communities

The chapter to date has concentrated on aspects of the use of digital technologies which support the practical connection and the networked connection of the connected professional. We shall now move on to their use in supporting the democratic and civic connections. The capacity of digital technology to build and support broader social networks has come to the fore in many ways across society, but using this capacity to extend education into working with the broader community has not received the attention or resources it deserves.

 *Spotlight on pedagogy*

Connecting communities

Lachapelle reviewed a number of research studies, and found that social networking 'has become a significant force in political organizing, social interaction, and economic development' (2011: 1). The dialoguing processes which can be facilitated by social networks have been seen to assist 'decision making, information sharing and relationship building in community development' (2011: 2). The acts of connection (literally) involved can help people build relationships through 'a shared community of interest' (2011: 2). A wider audience and community can be reached, and at their best, social networks can allow for broader participation, promote accountability, and operate to enhance openness and equality. It is of course possible that they could also do the opposite of those things when improperly used, and it is recognised that there is still a 'digital divide' between the haves and have nots in society.

There is, however, a significant potential for education in employing this use of digital technologies as one of our key tools to promote people-centred teaching. Lachapelle suggests that social media can promote community action and development best when:

- the tools involved remain easy to use

- professionals involved ensure they use, promote and exemplify responsible and ethical uses of social networking

- training in how to use social media and the digital devices involved is made available as a basic entitlement to communities and professionals alike

- developing network learning communities through the early use of acts of connection.

These ideas are just as applicable for teachers in FE.

Technology for all manifesto

Throughout this chapter we have seen that the use of digital technologies can leave us stranded in the digital swamp, or elevated to new possibilities in education and work in the community. There is no shortage, either, of examples of what doesn't work or examples of what does work, and advice is readily available (if you look) about how we can find positive ways out of the swamp and into active, deep network learning. Digital technologies really can help us to become connected professionals with engaged students, but some major shifts in policy and practice are needed for this to happen, and teachers need to be at the forefront of those changes.

When researching evidence of positive uses of digital technology, I discovered that there is a campaign (including of course a twitter hashtag) called 'maketechhuman'. The campaign has engagement from a large number of high profile organisations, individuals and companies, including Sir Stephen Hawking, Sir Tim Berners-Lee (the inventor of the World Wide Web), Nokia and many others. Up until the point of researching this book I have to admit that I had never heard of it, and it's possible you have not either. I do believe however that their message is very important.

 *Spotlight on pedagogy*

maketechhuman

One contribution to this campaign which is relevant was produced in April 2015 by Ian Wood, a senior partner at Lippincott (which is a 'global creative consultancy'). I can almost hear you all scoffing, but these ideas for a technology manifesto really are worth thinking about in efforts to make technology more human (or of course 'people-centred').

Three things are needed:

A movement

This would be 'a solid groundswell of opinion, strongly expressed. A voice not confined to techies and niches, that helps create clear expectations.' We do not want 'the human in the loop prioritising marketing objectives over human feelings' (Wood, 2015: 1).

Consequences

Wood argues that 'people have the power to change social norms, usually through the application of adverse consequences (social comment, loss of business etc.)' (2015: 1). Where there are negative and harmful uses of technology we have to stop them by using our own people and purchasing power. The movement created by making technology human could be a real focus for restraining the darker uses of technology.

Balance

We need to remember that 'a connected world is a wonderful thing. It should help people thrive every-where. We are not heading for disaster, we just need to keep our hands on the wheel' (Wood, 2015: 1).

Surely, some of the best people to contribute to and help to carry out this 'maketechhuman' manifesto are teachers. It's about time we were freed from the digital swamp and recognised as the people-centred professionals who can help achieve the true potential of digital technology.

 *Reflective learning exercise*

Act of connection – make your technology more human

To close, here are some maketechhuman guidelines based on the ideas in this chapter.

- Use technology to promote collaboration and community.
- Make sure any technology tools involved are easy to use.
- Model responsible and ethical uses of social networking with your students.
- Involve your students directly in making tech human.
- Get and give training and support in the use of digital technologies.
- Make use of what has already been learned about digital technologies.
- If it doesn't improve learning, say so!
- Start small and build through acts of connection.

Decide on and carry out one small act to avoid the digital swamp within the next month.

This chapter

This chapter has used the metaphor of the 'digital swamp' to highlight some of the challenges, issues and mistakes which education has already made, and continues to make when using digital technologies. Some strategies for managing and changing that situation in your own teaching and organisation were then introduced, including research evidence about what can and does work when using digital technologies in education. To help you to continue with your voyage out of the digital swamp, the chapter then addressed information overload and how to reduce it, followed by a more detailed consideration of network learning, with ideas about how to develop and introduce it. A consideration of using digital technologies as part of an FE teacher's civic connection in work with the community was included and the chapters closed with a 'technology for all manifesto' in the shape of a plea to 'maketechhuman'.

Notes for further reading

Higgins, S., Xiao, Z. and Katsipataki, M. (2012) *The impact of digital technology on learning: A summary for the Education Endowment Foundation*. Durham, UK: Education Endowment Foundation and Durham University.

You will be able to locate this report easily for download through an internet search of the title. Of the reviews of evidence about digital technology available, I think this is one of the clearest in its findings and recommendations. It is of course not about FE, but is relevant. The methodology is somewhat technical, but start by just reading up to page 5, and you will get some good further ideas there. Decide for yourself if you need to read any further.

Lachapelle, P. (2011) 'The use of social networking in community development'. *CD Practice*, 17, pp.1–8.

This is a concise and relatively low key journal article which addresses some useful and interesting ways in which digital technologies can help shape and support communities. It should give you some ideas and it is easy to read (unusual for journal articles). You can find it at:

> http://www.msucommunitydevelopment.org/paul/content/Lachapelle%202011%20The%20
> use%20of%20social%20networking%20in%20community%20development%20CD%20
> Practice.pdf

Veugelers, W. and O'Hair, M.J. (2005) *Network learning for educational change*. Maidenhead: Open University Press.

If you are interested in learning more about network learning, this book, which is a collection of 12 chapters on the theme by different authors, will take you through a variety of aspects of this approach to teaching and learning. Some of it is available as an electronic preview on Google books.

National Standards which are addressed by this chapter are:

1. Reflect on what works best in your teaching and learning to meet the diverse needs of learners.

2. Evaluate and challenge your practice, values and beliefs.

5. Value and promote social and cultural diversity, equality of opportunity and inclusion.

6. Build positive and collaborative relationships with colleagues and learners.

8. Maintain and update your knowledge of educational research to develop evidence-based practice.

15. Promote the benefits of technology and support learners in its use.

20. Contribute to organisational development and quality improvement through collaboration with others.

Chapter 6

Just teach 4 – Come together and stand together

Key learning points in this chapter

Education under the global spotlight

Mix and match – experience, reflection-in-action and reflection-on-action

The power of practitioner research – standing together and standing out

Working with the broader community

Spotlight on pedagogy

Education under the global spotlight

Education is one of the most important contributors globally to the progress and development of the human race. Governments around the world have grown to recognise this and have come together regularly in recent times to agree and review international aims, goals and targets for sustaining global education. In September 2015, a new Agenda for Sustainable Development was adopted by the international community with the intent to 'wipe out poverty' by 2030. The goals followed on from previous sets of goals, which had been partly successful, and were 'unanimously adopted by the 193 Member States of the United Nations who have the prime responsibility to realize them'

(Continued)

(Continued)

(UNESCO, 2017: 3). UNESCO reinforced the central role of education within this agenda with Goal 4 stating the aim to 'ensure inclusive and equitable quality education and promote lifelong learning opportunities for all' (UNESCO, 2017: 3). Some of the statistics cited by UNESCO bring home powerfully just how great the global education challenges are:

- 69 million new teachers are needed to reach the 2030 education goals

- 758 million adults (15% of all adults) lack any literacy skills: two thirds of whom are women

- $39 billion dollars of aid are needed to fill the annual education finance gap

- 263 million children and youth are out of school

- 14% of youth – and just 1% of the poorest girls – complete secondary education in low-income countries

- 35% of out-of-school children live in conflict-affected areas.

(UNESCO, 2017: 5)

Every teacher in the world is part of this global challenge. You may well say 'what has this got to do with me? I have enough on my plate with my local teaching situation here in the UK.' Don't believe that some of the problems of the world are irrelevant for our society. There are two good reasons why that is not the case.

Firstly there are major societal inequalities in the UK, and the Social Mobility Commission, an independent body that monitors progress on social mobility in the UK, has recently published a worrying report. The report finds strong evidence that 'two decades of government efforts to improve social mobility have failed to deliver enough progress in reducing the gap between Britain's haves and have nots' (Social Mobility Commission, 2017: 7). The gap is currently still increasing. The report gives 'red', 'amber' and 'green' ratings to what they described as 'four life stages', and the rating given depends on how successful public policy has been in terms of positive social outcomes' (2017: 2). The report comes to the shocking conclusion that firstly 'no life stage gets a green rating' (2017: 2). Disappointingly for a sector that works with many who are the less socially mobile, the 'young people and working lives' stage (the life stage including FE) 'receives a "red". Overall, only 7 policies score a "green" while 14 score "amber" and 16 "red"'. In simple terms, this means that inequality of life outcomes is still very much present in the UK, and that the FE sector has much to improve on if this is to change.

Secondly we are all global citizens. We can travel to almost anywhere in the world, communicate with almost anyone at any time, work and live almost anywhere and learn for free while we are there if we are of school age. We buy from global, instantly recognisable brands. Global citizenship is, however, about more than the internet, travel and work. UNESCO argues that global citizenship is about 'building and living in a peaceful world', and that education's role is to 'foster the knowledge, skills, values, attitudes and behaviours that allow individuals to take informed decisions and assume active roles locally, nationally and globally' (UNESCO, 2017: 2). As teachers in FE therefore we are part of a much bigger global context, and even our localised efforts make a difference to that global context.

Spotlight on pedagogy

PISA and its influence

Progress towards international educational goals has also seen the rise in international comparisons and ratings of education systems. One of the best known of these is the Programme for International Student Assessment (PISA) which is an international survey, carried out every three years, which aims to evaluate education systems worldwide. The method used is to give a large sample of 15 year olds a two-hour test, assessing their science, mathematics, reading, collaborative problem solving and financial literacy. PISA tests 'over half a million students, representing 28 million 15-year-olds in 72 countries and economies' (OECD, 2017). The results of the 2015 assessment were published on 6th December 2016. Overall, the UK was placed 15th out of the 72 countries involved in this, the most recent results. The PISA tests have been criticised as being an incomplete sample, and of lacking the scope needed to be fully valid, but governments pay very close attention to them, as do the media, and indeed schools. They do not relate directly to FE, but they certainly do indirectly. The education systems of whole countries have been changed to improve that country's PISA results, and much international educational capital is made by those who do well.

Reflective learning exercise

Going global

- In small groups, students research the education system of one other country. Each group can make their own choice of which country.
- Students should note four or five key points about the other systems then compare with the UK education system they have experienced to date.
- What is different and does it seem better than your experience?
- Use the results to ask 'should education be a global product?'

This activity can raise awareness of globalising features in education and promote a discussion, and can also be adapted and tailored to fit more subject-based teaching (e.g. 'how different do you think learning this subject might be in another country and why?').

We can see from this section that teaching is increasingly under a global spotlight. The global picture is important, but let's remind ourselves that the philosophy of this book is about starting small, and building from there with acts of connection. This includes finding sources of supportive advice and guidance, building your experience, and embracing the responsibilities involved without getting overwhelmed by it. One particularly helpful process is the use of what Donald Schon called 'reflection-in-action' and 'reflecting-on-action' (1983) you to adopt a 'mix and match' approach to your teaching.

Mix and match – experience, reflection-in-action and reflection-on-action

 Spotlight on pedagogy

Experience, reflection-in-action and reflection-on-action

Most of us hope that at some stage during our lives as teachers, someone will see us as a role model or even a 'great teacher'? Nesbit et al. suggest that great teachers 'think and act on a number of levels. Such teachers have a deep understanding of themselves and their students, and of the organisational contexts in which they work. They "think on their feet", and take a long term view of their work' (2004: 74). Aiming for these qualities and characteristics is within the grasp of all of us, but some advice about the way in which we can make progress towards being a great teacher is helpful. You will come across many ideas, educational fashions, situations and expectations as a teacher, and you will start to 'think on your feet' in the way described above as your experience grows, and this experience naturally develops your capacity to look further forward than the next teaching session. Although there are many outside influences and requirements, when you are in the room with your students you are the only person making the key decisions about how to engage them in their learning.

Donald Schon, argues that being a professional such as a teacher is more of an artistic endeavour than a technical operation, and he suggests that experience can help us to develop into someone like a talented musician, where we can improvise and be creative in our teaching in addition to using more routine capabilities to support that creativity and flexibility. Schon coined the term 'reflection-in-action' as the thinking on your feet which happens as you become more experienced, and 'reflecting-on-action' (Schon, 1983) as a more measured consideration of the teaching and surrounding events after the event. As you gain more experience you will begin to recognise more readily what has worked in teaching and what has not, and you will want to tweak or reinforce that to get as near as you can to an excellent session with deep student learning every time. Using 'reflection-in-action' and 'reflection-on-action' can help you to do that. At its simplest I would describe this as the 'mix and match' of teaching and learning. You have your own growing personal collection, or mix of teaching capabilities; you have a particular mix of students with their own individual and group needs; you have the curriculum which is intended, expected or required for that series of sessions; and you have your reflections on your growing experience of teaching to help you judge how to proceed.

This is a process of mix and match. If you can trust your own developing professional judgement to decide how you mix and match those components and if this mix does bring positive results with your students, you are on the way to finding the key to successful teaching. If you have one or two frameworks to focus and accelerate the learning process within your attempts to mix and match, that will help. The use of 'critical reflection' can be particularly helpful. Yvonne Hillier (2002: xi) is clear when she states 'without critical reflection, teaching will remain at best uninformed, and at worst ineffective, prejudiced and constraining'. Critical reflection is developed when we question 'our routine, convenient, everyday practices and ask ourselves about what really does and doesn't work'. This will 'challenge our taken for granted assumptions' (Hillier, 2002: 7) about what we feel, think and do.

Act of connection – into the mix with critical reflection

Reflect on a recent incident, activity or resource from your teaching, for example:

- You have developed a supporting website for one of your subjects and groups of students, and all of the materials from your teaching sessions, and a range of other support materials are now all there, organised week by week.

- Over the course of the year, some students make reference to them, and the site is getting some visits, but when you compare your students' attendance and achievement from this year and last, there is no improvement since this website has gone live.

This would not raise any major red lights for you in terms of results, but you would naturally wonder why the resource does not seem to have had an impact. To critically reflect on this incident, you would need to ask some challenging questions:

- Did I ask the students what they feel will help them improve their results before creating the website?
- Did I think about what students could get from the website?
- Did I create it because I enjoy using technology?
- What could I do differently and why?

The results of this piece of critical reflection could well provide you with a number of ways of solving the problem you have identified. It may even make you ask some of the questions before using a resource or activity which was suggested in Chapter 5. It should certainly help you to mix your teaching activities to more successfully match your students' needs. As with many of the acts of connection in this book, this should provide you with small, recognisable gains in the classroom and in your students' learning. If you critically reflect regularly it can go beyond this into helping you develop that 'thinking ahead' which is part of being a great people-centred teacher.

The power of practitioner research – standing together and standing out

One way of taking critical reflection further than considering small incidents in your teaching is to get involved in research. When and how can a busy FE teacher get involved in research? However busy teachers are, they always carry out research at some level as a normal part of their job. Whether it is to keep their subject up to date, to prepare a teaching session, for continuing professional development or to gain qualifications all teachers and indeed all professionals need to carry out research. It may not be more academic research involving projects and write-ups, but the general techniques and motivation are the same and research to improve your teaching and the achievements of your students will always be useful. The conditions of service and circumstances of FE don't exactly make finding time and resources for research easy, but in my experience teachers are natural enquirers (as are their students). I have worked on and with small and large projects involving practitioner research with thousands of FE teachers and their students over the last 40 years, and have often been in awe of their determination and persistence. FE teachers and their other colleagues can remain engaged, enthusiastic and determined to find out something useful for their teaching and learning through research, even within an often less than helpful environment.

 Spotlight on pedagogy

Practitioner research as empowerment

Duckworth (2016: 35) describes practitioner research as a 'tool for empowerment' which can 'build a meaningful approach to . . . professional (and indeed personal) development; it has the potential to shift teachers from passive receivers of knowledge to the generators of knowledge.' It can also produce a 'ripple effect that touches and empowers . . . students and the community' (2016: 36).

Individuals and groups can be empowered by researching their own practice, and that of others, and they could be described as carrying out a series of interconnected acts of connection when carrying out their own research, but even more so when working with others. There is good evidence, which has already been represented in this book, that collaboration and joint working, or 'standing together to stand out' can achieve more than working alone.

 Spotlight on pedagogy

Joint Practice Development

By way of an example, one of the currently popular approaches to teacher and institutional development is 'Joint Practice Development' (JPD). JPD makes use of research to work towards progress and improvement in teaching and learning across institutions, organisations, teams and individuals through collaboration. Joint Practice Development is defined by Sebba et al. as 'the process of learning new ways of working through mutual engagement that opens up and shares practices with others' (2010: 2). Sebba et al.'s 2010 review of evidence about the value of JPD (based on schools, but relevant to FE) found that 'mutual learning, development and exchange of knowledge' had clearly taken place. They offered a structure which would help to support the process of standing together to help the work of those participating to stand out.

 Reflective learning exercise

Act of connection – researching with others

Here is a useful checklist which you can use when considering taking part in or initiating collaborative research or JPD. Ensure that you:

- Consider what research has already been undertaken in this field and learn from that
- Set clear aims and improvement priorities
- Develop trust across all taking part
- Build on existing relationships and networks
- Develop new networks where needed
- Establish leadership which works with and across all levels of activity
- Build in challenge and support for teachers and students
- Decide on activities with genuine local relevance to all involved
- Build in student participation at all stages
- Design and carry out your own evaluation.

 Spotlight on pedagogy

JPD in action – examples from FE

There are many good examples available of individual teachers, groups of teachers, teams and organisations standing together and standing out, and one featured in Chapter 5 in relation to uses of technology, which was the Clean Break project. Two more examples of small teacher research projects follow.

The Teacher Education for Specialist Teachers (TEST) project

The TEST project established and made use of a collaborative partnership between a national development organisation for Teacher Education, the Association for Centres of Excellence in Teacher Training (ACETT); three of its regional members, LONCETT in the London area, SUCCESS NORTH in the north east and SWCETT in the south west; a specialist Special Educational Needs College (National Star College), and Bath Spa University's Teacher Education team. The project aimed to:

- identify and evaluate current practice in the training of Special Educational Needs (SEN)/ Learning Disability and/or Difficulty (LDD) teacher educators
- develop, run and evaluate a CPD programme to support their development needs
- make recommendations for future training.

From the project final report, it can be seen that all the necessities for good quality JPD listed above were present in this project. The achievements and outcomes of the project included:

- successfully recruiting and running a CPD programme which was very well evaluated by participants, as were the associated resources
- highlighting the lack of available specialist SEN/LDD teacher education

(Continued)

(Continued)

- establishing a new network of SEN practitioners in the North

- learning from the research how to move forward from existing practice.

One comment from a participant strongly indicates the spirit and value of the programme:

> participants were excited about the prospect of developing models within their own organisa-
> tions and, as a CPD activity, had found the three days to be beneficial and enjoyable. They
> particularly valued the opportunity to share experiences and to discuss their needs - course
> leader. (ACETT, 2015: 8)

This project is a good example of work which helps teachers make connections, stand together, and
stand out.

 Reflective learning exercise

Act of connection - getting ideas for practitioner research

If you are encouraged by the examples above to get involved in research using JPD or another
approach, it is possible to both make and take opportunities to do so. A simple activity follows which
can help you decide what a small project may focus on.

Ask yourself these questions (this can work better if you discuss it with a colleague):

- What themes or topics to do with my teaching would I like to find out more about?
- What could I try out which may be new and worthwhile?
- What evidence about that theme or topic is already available that I can learn from?
- What aims could the joint research have?
- Who else would I like to work with?
- Where might I get some funding from?
- How can I involve my students?
- What actions or activities could be involved?
- What methods could I use to try out new approaches and solutions?
- How do I ensure any conclusions are fair and accurate?
- How will I know if this research is making a difference?
- How could we embed the results in our teaching?
- Who else could I share what I am doing with?

The results of these questions should give you some good project ideas to work on.

Spotlight on pedagogy

Working with the broader community

The last example of practitioner research is an example of a college reaching out into, and working with, its local community with benefits to all involved. In 2011, the Independent Commission on Colleges in their Communities (UK) published its report. I'm not sure many readers will know about it, as it unfortunately had little impact at the time or since. The report investigated the broader role of colleges in the community, and came to some significant conclusions. Be reminded also that colleges are only part of our definition of the FE sector, so this was always a report which lacked evidence from the full breadth of the sector. Many other parts of FE work on an ongoing basis in and with the broader community. Charities and community organisations are also often involved as learning providers. The report found that 'colleges can not only help people into jobs through skills training, but, by being proactive in their work with local communities, can also harness the energy of those communities towards positive outcomes which in turn promote health, happiness and social cohesion' (2011: 3). The findings of the commission should have been significant. Colleges could, and should be

> a 'dynamic nucleus' at the heart of their communities, promoting a shared agenda of activities which both fulfil their central role of providing learning and skills training to young people and adults, but also reach out into their communities, catalysing a whole range of further activities. We see the college as the central player in a network of partnerships, dynamic in the sense of developing and engaging with other partners. This enables the network itself to become part of the dynamic, with colleges at its heart. (2011: 4)

Sadly this report has largely been ignored, but it does remind us of the 'democratic connection and civic connection' of the connected professional, or 'active participation in civic action with the wider community to support development with and for that community' (see Chapter 1).

FE does still have many connections with the community and, as the final example of practitioner research in the chapter shows, does already work with the broader community.

Spotlight on pedagogy

Community ESOL Conversation clubs

Thurrock Adult Community College (TACC) took part in an Education and Training Foundation funded 'Outstanding Teaching, Learning and Assessment' (OTLA) project (as was the case in the Clean Break project which featured in Chapter 5) in 2015. The project aimed to establish a wider engagement with minority communities in Thurrock and used English as a Second or Other Language (ESOL) activities to reduce their isolation and help them to develop their English language skills. These projects encouraged participants to think outside of their institution, and TACC established links with local voluntary

(Continued)

(Continued)

and community sector organisations who were already working with minority communities and this built into a working partnership for this project. As a result of this collaboration, a series of 'ESOL Conversation Clubs' were established as an informal means of supporting and developing ESOL, and a number of ESOL volunteers were trained in order to host the clubs. The project has proved to be a fruitful collaboration between advanced ESOL learners who volunteered to host the clubs, the college specialist teaching team and the organisations already working with the minority groups. A number of clubs have been established and evaluated, and participants found them both socially enjoyable and helpful with their English. This is another smaller scale and at the time of writing not yet fully developed piece of JPD, which again shows the value of standing together to stand out.

Working with your local community is the ultimate statement of standing together and standing out, so this chapter closes with an act of connection which can help you to map your college, your subject and your own connections with the community and think about how they could be taken forward.

Reflective feature

Act of connection – switching on the civic connection

For this activity an inclusive definition of the community is used which includes defined community groups, clubs, businesses, public sector organisations and other educational organisations.

Working with other colleagues from your organisation, list or map visually what you would consider to be civic connections between your department, college, training provider, voluntary organisation or other educational provider which you know of or already exist by asking:

- What connections do we already have within the community through work? (E.g. collaborations with businesses; volunteering with charities; partnerships with sports clubs for training, facilities and work experience ... there are many civic connections.)
- What connections do we already have within the community outside work?
- How do they link in to our teaching and our organisation?
- What benefits are there for us, our students, our organisation and the broader community?
- What more could we do?

When this activity is done, participants are usually surprised to see that civic connections already exist to a larger degree than they thought, and that many colleges are more embedded in their community than they may think. Although the 'dynamic nucleus' vision has not been fulfilled, many FE organisations are embedded strongly in their local community, and this is often helped by their activities where they stand together and stand out.

This chapter

This chapter firstly examined a number of the ways in which education is in the global spotlight, but then related that to inequality in our own country, and how important it is for FE to have improving social mobility at its heart. With a more directly practical focus, the chapter then considered how critical reflection, and in particular Schon's ideas about 'reflection-in-action' and 'reflection-on-action' can help teachers 'mix and match' their teaching choices, strategies and approaches to best suit the situation they are working in and the needs of their students. Examples of practitioner research were then introduced, where FE teachers stand together to stand out, and develop new practices and principles of teaching, and the argument was built that this type of research can be a significantly empowering process for teachers and students. This penultimate chapter closed with an appeal to all to broaden the civic connections in their working lives so that the transformative benefits of people-centred teaching in FE can extend to all.

Notes on further reading

Education and Training Foundation (2017) *Outstanding teaching, learning and assessment.* [online] http://www.et-foundation.co.uk/supporting/support-practitioners/improvements-in-teacher-learning-and-assessment/ accessed 16/7/17.

This is an online resource of reports, outputs and data from a range of 'Outstanding Teaching, Learning and Assessment' projects. Take a good browse around, and you will almost certainly find a project which is relevant to you.

Social Mobility Commission (2017) Time for change: An assessment of government policies on social mobility 1997–2017. London: Social Mobility Commission.

This organisation does an excellent job at reporting in and arguing how education can enhance and improve social mobility, but this report clearly shows just how big a challenge this is, even in such a rich country as the UK.

UNESCO (2017) *Education transforms lives.* Paris: United Nations Educational, Scientific and Cultural Organization.

You will be able to get this document easily with an internet search. If you are interested in finding out more about global education, this publication should be one of your first stops. UNESCO 'as the sole UN agency mandated to cover all aspects of education and with a worldwide network of specialized institutes and offices, is entrusted to lead and coordinate the achieving of this goal with its partners through the Education 2030 Agenda'.

National Standards which are addressed by this chapter are:

1. Reflect on what works best in your teaching and learning to meet the diverse needs of learners.

2. Evaluate and challenge your practice, values and beliefs.

4. Be creative and innovative in selecting and adapting strategies to help learners to learn.

5. Value and promote social and cultural diversity, equality of opportunity and inclusion.

6. Build positive and collaborative relationships with colleagues and learners.

7. Maintain and update knowledge of your subject and/or vocational area.

8. Maintain and update your knowledge of educational research to develop evidence-based practice.

9. Apply theoretical understanding of effective practice in teaching, learning and assessment drawing on research and other evidence.

10. Evaluate your practice with others and assess its impact on learning.

19. Maintain and update your teaching and training expertise and vocational skills through collaboration with employers.

20. Contribute to organisational development and quality improvement through collaboration with others.

Part 3
Just keep teaching

Chapter 7

Just keep teaching – teaching and learning careers

 Key learning points in this chapter

Resilience and positive growth

Managing the three Ps

Don't let OfSTED lurk in the background

Learning careers and teaching careers

Glancing to the future of teaching

Help the human race – be a people-centred teacher

This chapter brings us to the end of our journey into people-centred teaching. It starts by introducing why resilience is needed by teachers and their students, and suggests that a 'growth mindset' can help to develop this important quality. This is followed by practical advice to assist with managing some of the day-to-day pressures of teaching in FE and suggestions for preparing for inspection by 'getting inside' Ofsted. Next, opportunities to reflect on how to work on developing successful 'learning careers' with your students and how teachers can achieve lengthy 'teaching careers' are both provided. The book closes with a reminder of the key ideas, thinking and advice about what constitutes a people-centred teacher. A book such as this would not be complete without a final rallying call to all teachers to strive to be people-centred, and that is indeed how the book closes.

Resilience, reinforcement and reassurance

Katherine Weare provides us with a good definition of resilience, when she states that resilience involves the ability to:

- 'bounce back' after an upset or lack of success

- be flexible and adaptive in our response to a problem

- process and learn from a difficult experience, and use it to aid our own development and learning

- move on rather than be immobilised by upset or failure

- keep trying when it gets tough.

(Adapted from Weare, 2004: 40.)

 *Spotlight on pedagogy*

A growth mindset

Resilience is a necessary characteristic in life and is particularly important in teaching.

This is partly because the going can get tough, but also because teaching is demanding, mentally and physically, and resilience will help you to maintain the energy and commitment you need. Our students also need to be resilient. When multiple assessment deadlines are approaching, resilience is a vitally important quality for students, and can be a key factor in helping them to succeed. One approach to developing resilience can be found in Carol Dweck's ideas about a 'growth mindset'. Dweck's research, outlined in her 2006 book, argues that there are two attitudes to learning which manifest themselves as one of two 'mindsets', either a 'fixed mindset' or 'growth mindset' (Dweck, 2006). A fixed mindset is not necessarily something that leads to poor learning, but is, as the name suggests, fixed in its approach, with a lack of agility and flexibility. Dweck argues that those with a fixed mindset thrive on success because it confirms their own self-concept, but that they are likely to fear failure, not take on challenging tasks and, as a result, not grow as much from learning as they could. Those with a growth mindset on the other hand believe that hard work and perseverance will help them and their learning to grow, and they tend to be prepared to take risks and make mistakes but will still keep going to achieve their goals and improvement in their learning.

Those with a growth mindset tend to have both strong self-belief and resilience. Reinforcement and reassurance are both important aspects of nurturing a growth mindset. Pleasance (2016), when introducing some of Dweck's ideas, summarises what teachers need to do to develop a 'growth mindset learning environment', so that it will help their students' self-belief:

- Believe in all your students

- Create a 'can do' ethos

- Make a safe space for students to make mistakes

- Ensure that students value their learning
- Foster opportunities for students to overcome challenges
- Help students to develop resilience
- Praise effort.

(Adapted from Pleasance, 2016: 51.)

 Reflective learning exercise

Act of connection – growing my resilience

This exercise uses Weare's (2004) ideas about resilience to provide questions you can ask about your own mindset, and discuss with at least one other colleague.

- How do you 'bounce back' after an upset or lack of success?
- Are you flexible in your response to a problem?
- How do you learn from a difficult experience, and use it to aid your own development and learning?
- What strategies do you use to move on rather than be immobilised by upset or failure?
- How do you keep trying when it gets tough?

 Reflective learning exercise

Act of connection – growing my students' resilience

How do you help your students to develop resilience and a growth mindset?

- Do you clearly show that you really believe in all your students? If so how and why, and if not how and why not?
- Do you have a 'can do' ethos?
- Are your teaching spaces safe places for students to make mistakes?
- How do you ensure that students value their learning?
- How do you foster opportunities for students to overcome challenges?
- How do you help learners to develop resilience?
- Do you praise effort?
- Which of these things would you like to change first, and how can you get some help to do it?

(Continued)

> (Continued)
>
> As has been said throughout the book, make sure you record any actions or developments proposed, as you don't want to lose them.
>
> There are many exercises available online to help develop and use a growth mindset, and I have seen them used recently extensively with students as the focus of a collaborative FE project between three institutions. The use of curriculum planning and learning activities to promote a growth mindset worked particularly well, and the project outputs and outcomes demonstrated a significant impact on students and their achievements.

Managing the three Ps

In my 2010 book, *In at the Deep End* (Crawley, 2010), I used the idea of 'the three Ps' as 'the most persistent pressures you face in your work as a teacher' (2010: 123). The three Ps are the three types of pressure I argued were pervasive in the work of FE teachers, and they are paper, people and personal pressures. These are still very much present now, so I am returning to them and refreshing them.

Paper pressure

Despite our considerably greater adoption of and, indeed, immersion in digital technology (as discussed in Chapter 5), electronic paper pressure has tended to draw us further into the 'digital swamp' rather than liberating us from routine tasks. Much physical paper also still crosses or piles on our desks (if of course we still have desks) every day. Paper pressure is endemic in FE.

People pressure

People pressure, where you interact professionally with students, managers, other teachers, internal and external verifiers, and outside interests and communities (i.e. people) is also intense. In education systems across the world, it appears that teachers are seen as the solutions to all the problems in the world, and this is in addition to their 'normal' work of teaching and supporting the learning and achievement of their students.

Personal pressure

There is often a lot of pressure on you as an individual. Personal pressure is about how you personally manage all of these pressures associated with your work and your life.

There is already practical advice about how to manage the three Ps scattered throughout the book (in Chapters 4, 5 and 6 for example), and it is essentially about having a strong, resilient and positive self-concept, and being able to remain calm, assured, engaged and assertive under pressure. In the immortal words of Douglas Adams, one of your key mottos should be:

> Don't panic. (Adams, 1979: 2)

Another activity I provided in 2010 is still what I would recommend as a personal energiser for all teachers at all stages of their careers, so it is provided here in an updated version.

Reflective learning exercise

Act of connection – challenging your mindset

This activity is a part of the journey towards developing resilience and a growth mindset. The following self-assessment questions are based on Clow and Palmer (2004). Don't try to ask all of the questions all at once, or take all the possible actions at once as it is likely that this would overload you. Use them when you need to and they can be very helpful in taking the type of small steps which have been encouraged throughout the book towards managing the three Ps and maintaining positivity and energy.

- Challenge awfulising beliefs – am I making a mountain out of a molehill and turning 'life hassle' into 'life horror'?
- Challenging 'I can't stand it-itis' – Will this part of my work really be that bad? I've found positive solutions before so why would I not now?
- Challenging global ratings of the self or others – Do I really rate as a failure (or 'unsatisfactory') because of one negative event?

Managing the three Ps is all about self-belief, working hard to improve and judging your own professional self as fairly as you judge your students. Small steps towards a growth mindset could prove to be big steps away from a fixed mindset.

Don't let Ofsted lurk in the background

Spotlight on pedagogy

Ofsted and FE

Inspections of FE providers began in 1993 under the auspices of the Further Education Funding Council, and from 2000 Ofsted took over inspections of college provision for young people while the Adult Learning Inspectorate (ALI) was created to inspect adult provision in colleges, work-based learning and community learning. Inspections were joint operations between the two agencies with varying levels of success.

(Continued)

(Continued)

In 2007, Ofsted took over from ALI, and a single inspectorate has been inspecting FE ever since. Inspection frameworks across the different phases of education have only converged recently. Over my teaching career, I have experienced inspection, either as a teacher or a course leader (or both), on a total of four occasions, and each one has been accompanied an increased degree of stress, pressure and paperwork. The most recent inspection was in 2011, and it was of the FE teacher education programme I was leading. It was a very successful outcome. I now teach only on programmes (Education Studies) which are not at present inspected by Ofsted and the difference is significant in terms of the reduction of day-to-day stress. This alone is a major indictment of the Ofsted process.

The amount of work for all involved in preparing for Ofsted has grown exponentially since inspections were first introduced, to the point where it now has to become almost an obsession if individuals and organisations are to do well. Even if you do well, you do not end up feeling that all the work and stress is worth it. The stress and time involved in Ofsted preparation can be greatly damaging to teachers, students, organisations and, in the final analysis, education, irrespective of the results. It is simply not fair to exert that much stress on hard-working professionals.

Positively managing inspections

Is it possible to manage Ofsted, do well, and remain a people-centred teacher? Let's consider what inspections are supposed to be about. Few would disagree with the goal of Ofsted which is 'to achieve excellence in education and skills for learners of all ages, and in the care of children and young people' (Ofsted, 2017a). Few would disagree with establishing good practice through comparing different organisations, initiatives and sector themes. What then turns these worthwhile aims into such a flawed process?

Spotlight on pedagogy

What are Ofsted's criteria for success?

Let's take a close look at the current Ofsted criteria for success. These do change, but they still tend to address the same key areas. Inside the 71 pages of the 2017 Inspector's Handbook for FE, you will find the 'grade descriptors' for 'outstanding quality of teaching, learning and assessment' (Ofsted, 2017b: 43). There are many other criteria for other aspects of teaching and learning, but these are the ones which all teachers would probably set their sights on first if asked. The handbook does regularly change, but if you search for 'further education inspector's handbook', that should take you to the most current version. I have translated the criteria below into the most straightforward language I can (not an Ofsted strength). Don't forget that these are the hallmarks of 'outstanding teaching'. To be considered outstanding, there would need to be evidence from the inspection of:

- Curious and highly engaged students who are thriving in their learning.

- Students who are self-improving with the help of high quality support from staff.

- Determined, well qualified and motivational teachers who have high expectations and set high targets working with their students.

- Learning sessions which are planned to challenge students to realise their potential, provide deep progressing learning and include support for student needs.

- Assessment information and feedback which engages students in improving their learning and moving on to the next stages.

- Engagement with parents and/or employers which helps teachers and others to support the students' learning.

- An environment in which equality and inclusion is actively pursued to recognise and value diversity and enhance students' understanding of people and communities.

- High quality teaching and promotion of English, maths, ICT and employability skills.

(Based on Ofsted, 2017a: 43.)

It may be something of an over-simplification, but these key principles of teaching and learning which Ofsted describe do broadly align with the principles of people-centred teaching outlined in this book. Unfortunately, the time spent collecting and organising evidence for inspections means that the whole process has become a bureaucratic juggernaut which is now in urgent need of reform. Frank Coffield argues that FE is 'too important and too expensive to be evaluated by a model of inspection that is not fit for the future' (Coffield, 2017: ii).

How then can we be people-centred teachers, and still do well in Ofsted inspections? Do we actually want to? The fact is that you cannot just try to get on with your teaching and not think of Ofsted at all (or at least very few people in the sector can). The main problem is not what we are asked to do in terms of gathering evidence, but rather the degree to which gathering the evidence has become a dominant force across FE which pushes out other at least as important aspects of education. The time spent preparing for Ofsted genuinely makes preparing and carrying out your regular day-to-day teaching much more difficult. If you lead a programme or run a department, the work is literally never-ending. I have been on holiday with boxes of Ofsted paperwork in our car; I've cancelled holidays because of Ofsted and created systems for classroom observation for our course that have been pragmatically based on satisfying what Ofsted required. Our team did not believe in it, but we decided we had to do it.

How to manage an inspection

What then is the best way to manage an inspection? The key is to get inside the world of Ofsted, and align (not force) the best bits of your own teaching with their criteria and expectations. In other words you develop and reinforce what you believe is outstanding in what you do and match it to Ofsted requirements. This is not easy, but if you can demonstrate that your students consistently achieve high quality deep learning and how you help that, it will meet many of the criteria for an outstanding result. This also fits well within the notion considered in Chapter 6 of 'mix and match'.

Act of connection - owning outstanding

To manage Ofsted you firstly need to be confident about yourself as a teacher/organiser/manager. As has been already said in this book, you need trust, empathy, motivation, positivity, determination, resilience and self-belief. It helps if you also have feedback from others that suggests you are at least a good teacher. How many of the following suggestions you need to take on board will depend on your position and role as a teacher, course leader, subject leader, department leader etc. You need to:

- Prioritise relational leadership - when all are working towards the same goal and all take a share in the work and decisions about quality you will have motivation across a team which can develop what are described as 'self-improving systems'.

- Get inside Ofsted - find the handbooks for FE inspections and get familiar with the language and criteria. Treat it like getting to know a new syllabus (although it will be one of the least user-friendly you will have come across). Read inspection reports of other organisations like your own. Go as far as you feel you need to with this, but knowing what you are dealing with is essential.

- Translate Ofsted speak - find ways (working with colleagues is good for this) of creating teaching documents which are both useable by your team, make sense to your students, and reflect Ofsted criteria. This can help to provide more motivational lessons, more challenging learning and more people-centred support for your students.

- Experience mock inspections - devise your own mock inspection sessions across your team where you all inspect each other (just another name for peer learning really) so that you get used to the process, the evidence and the routine.

- Call in expert advice - you may or not have the money to pay for this, but find out if there are teachers in other departments or even other establishments who have done well in Ofsted and see if you can visit them, or get them to visit you to share and swap experience.

- Don't forget your students - make sure your students are also involved in decisions about what to change and improve. Evidence about what your students have learned is the cornerstone of all inspections. If your students have a high opinion of their learning and of your teaching that is really important as it is exactly what Ofsted want to see.

- Make real improvements - don't do things just because Ofsted want it. If you decide on improvements and the evidence of learning and achievement is at least good, that is what makes the difference, and Ofsted will appreciate that.

- Organise your evidence - make sure that the administrative system you use for gathering and organising evidence results in a clear and transparent set of documents, artefacts and records. All evidence needs to be easy for Ofsted to find, and for you to use.

- Pay attention to detail at every stage - this does get somewhat tedious, but keep checking your results and fine tuning what you do where you need to. If someone asks you a detailed question about evidence you need to be able to answer it with the evidence quickly available.

- A strong team ethos - at times this is what carries you all through. It's like all being in it together, and this tends to bring out the best in open and supportive teams. Given the encouragement, people work well in teams, and this also spreads the workload.

Learning careers and teaching careers

Martin Bloomer and Phil Hodkinson used FE-based research to develop the idea that young people's 'perceptions of and approaches to learning' (Bloomer and Hodkinson, 2000: 583) and the way that they develop over time could be described as 'learning careers'.

 Spotlight on pedagogy

Learning careers

Bloomer and Hodkinson's work was instrumental in influencing a wide range of decisions and actions about supporting students in FE which have developed over the nearly 20 years since their research was published, so it is worth spending a little time on explaining what research they carried out, and what they concluded from that research.

When reviewing research on learning they were surprised to find that few 'related learning to broader social and economic patterns'. Their own longitudinal study 'tracked 50 young people from the final year of their English secondary education, aged 15/16, into FE and beyond' (2000: 585). There were 289 interviews carried out with the participants, who also included school and college teachers and parents, and the fieldwork was completed when most of the students were aged 19 or 20 years. The data showed that the young people changed in the way they viewed learning depending on the time and situation of their lives. As the data from students accumulated 'we found that existing theories about learning were inadequate for the purpose of making sense of what we were finding. We have therefore developed the concept of learning careers' (Bloomer and Hodkinson, 2000: 590). The term 'learning career' explains how learning changes and develops for people as they change and develop as people. As their experiences of life change, this influences their disposition to learning and may well change what and when they learn.

In essence, the notion appears straightforward when you think about it. The time people spend in education has a major effect on their learning, particularly when they spend so much of their time in education in their younger formative years. Education is not however the only influence on people's learning and, depending on their life situation, may not be the strongest influence at any given time. This research was used to help FE organisations and the sector as a whole develop support systems for students which could mitigate the issues and challenges they faced outside of education so that the learning they gained inside FE could be more effectively undertaken. Their research was not the only factor which led to learning support becoming an important function of FE, but supporting students' learning careers did become a significant part of the work of FE teachers and others.

 Reflective learning exercise

Act of connection – positive learning careers

This is an activity which can work well with teachers and students. It starts with participants working individually, and then in small groups to share their individual results.

(Continued)

(Continued)

- How would you describe your 'learning career'?
- What are the key positive and negative moments to date? Draw them as a timeline.
- List three things that have helped the positive aspects and three things that have created the negative moments of your learning career.
- What are the most important things now to help your learning career to be positive?
- How can your teachers, your family, friends and fellow students help this to happen?

 Spotlight on pedagogy

Teaching careers

If students have learning careers, teachers must have them too. These have been called 'teaching careers', the 'teaching journey' and 'teaching career phases' to name but a few. Huberman (1989) produced one of the best-known theories about what happens to a teacher over their career, and he suggested there are five stages involved. These are:

- Career entry – the teacher often feels a novice who at times struggles to survive; wonders how others manage the work, and gets through on a day-to-day basis.
- Stabilisation – the teacher is starting to cope, and feels like they are both 'getting the hang of it', being able to concentrate more on their students rather than their teaching, and are starting to try out changes and improvements.
- Experimentation – the teacher moves towards becoming an 'expert' teacher; manages learning with consistency and is ready to take on challenges and try something new.
- Conservatism – they may start to see the path chosen as a teacher as stagnating with less or little to look forward to. Something like a 'mid-life crisis' can be experienced.
- Disengagement or expert – as they look towards the end of their career they may look for opportunities to disengage from responsibility and make way for others. They may also reach an expert level where their wealth of experience is a great asset to their students and their organisation.

Huberman did not see these stages as static and argued that there could be variation in the timing of the stages, whether they all happen in every teacher's career, whether teachers revert to 'earlier' stages or remain in a single stage during a career. What he did do, however, is produce some ideas which can help us as teachers to reflect on where we are, where we may wish to be, and how we can get there.

Act of connection - your teaching career

Which of Huberman's (1989) stages are you at, or have you visited?

- career entry
- stabilisation
- experimentation
- conservatism
- disengagement or expert.

Where do you see yourself in terms of your teaching career over the next three to five years?

How will you get there, what help do you need, and where will you get that help?

Which small step or steps will you start with?

Glancing towards the future of teaching

We are coming towards the end of our journey in this book, and it is time to think about the future of teaching, and where you may fit in that future. Publications about the future of education and/or teaching appear regularly. If you have read any of these they will almost certainly contain ideas about technology transforming learning and education, about 'world class' schooling and about preparing our populations for work in a global society. They often gaze into a future where:

- teachers 'flip' learning
- students sign in and sign out of their personalised learning programmes as they need to
- teaching takes place in 'student hubs'
- teachers are the highly skilled supporters of this process, dragging and dropping learning material into a student's drop box
- teachers are enjoying their high social status as teachers and their refreshed work/life balance.

This is of course possible and in some respects desirable, but as we have suggested in Chapter 5, there are considerable flaws in the argument which tends to treat technology as the solution rather than a learning tool. I have been using technology in my teaching since about 1983, and the main problem has been keeping up with the newest software and hardware, and finding the time to really make the most of the tools offered. We certainly need to change, and even transform the FE sector, but it is a mistake to think that technology itself will be the main vehicle on the journey to a better future. There are much bigger priorities.

Spotlight on pedagogy

A dynamic and inclusive future for further education

What then would be a positive, people-centred vision of the future of Further Education? Andy Hargreaves is another current educational thinker who often has things to say which are worth reading. Back as far as 2003 he was arguing that teaching needed to be transformed, and that the future of teachers was to 'help build a social movement for a dynamic and inclusive system of public education in the knowledge society by

- Rekindling their own moral missions and purposes in a system that has begun to lose sight of them.

- Opening their actions and minds to parents and communities and engaging with their missions.

- Working with their unions to become agents of their own change, not just opponents of change proposed by others.

- Courageously speaking out against injustice and exclusion wherever they see it.

- Recognising that they have a professional responsibility not just to their own children, but also to other people's children, in chains of care.

Hargreaves (2003: 206)

For a more recently published perspective on the future of teaching, Michael Fullan and Andy Hargreaves produced a report entitled 'Call to action - Bringing the Profession Back in' in 2016. They articulately explain how evidence demonstrates that the quality of teaching is the most important factor in education which affects student learning and achievement. They passionately assert that 'becoming a teacher is about moral purpose. It is about teachers' commitment to an agenda focused on equity and making a positive difference to children's lives' (Fullan and Hargreaves, 2016: 2). They then lay out how they believe the teaching profession needs to be 'brought back in' and allowed to 'lead the development of practice' through being 'deeply rooted in a learning culture' which is localised and focused on equality (2016: 2).

Spotlight on pedagogy

Bringing the professional back into FE

The two measures recommended by Fullan and Hargreaves (2016) are included here as part of the closing argument of this book because of their particular relevance to the future of teaching in FE.

Improving student and teacher well-being

Fullan and Hargreaves chart how 'good old pedagogies' such as the ideas of John Dewey and Carl Rogers have become buried and pushed into the background 'with a global education reform movement that standardized and prescribed the curriculum, and turned what were once humanistic and inclusive classrooms into test-preparation factories' (2016: 15). This process, plus more students becoming disengaged from education, global refugee crises and a worldwide spread of mental health problems has pushed deep, engaged, people-centred learning to the back of the agenda. This can be clearly seen as a problem within FE. Throughout this book, a variety of strategies and activities have been featured focusing on developing FE teachers' capacity to enhance the well-being of their students, and their own well-being.

Using 'good new pedagogies'

There are also however 'good new pedagogies' which can 'engage and energize and teachers as well as students and promote their joint learning and development' (Fullan and Hargreaves, 2016: 15). They are often 'student-driven' and 'activist' because in good new pedagogies, students have a voice and can become campaigners and agents of change. Given a voice they can take responsibility for their own learning, ask difficult questions and collaborate. When encouraged to develop their own 'civic connection' students can take up personal, local, national and even international causes.

Good new pedagogies also 'make positive uses of digital technology' (Fullan and Hargreaves, 2016: 17). Live activity, real-time feedback and ongoing online interaction with each other and others which is largely self-managed can also deepen engagement and learning. Students could be and should be a vital resource in the positive uses of digital technology, and teachers need to do much more to help students lead the way.

Overall, a combination of these two measures would have a powerful impact on the teaching profession. 'Having more student engagement and student voice, engaged in activist and other projects that provide continuous and honest feedback online and offline, is a powerful stimulator for teachers' well-being' (Fullan and Hargreaves, 2016: 17). It is also a powerful contributor to student well-being.

 Reflective learning exercise

Act of connection – building the future for all teachers

How then can we move towards this more positive future for teaching? One of the final acts of connection in the book takes Fullan and Hargreaves' call for action and adapts it as a set of recommendations for all teachers in FE.

These actions are not in any order of priority, and can be undertaken and combined in any informal, structured, personal or collaborative way from which you will gain value.

- Find opportunities to collaborate with other professionals – connecting with other teachers, with students, with communities and with others through network learning will make a difference. You have to take the initiative.

(Continued)

> *(Continued)*
>
> - Work to find deep learning wherever and whenever you can - with the good new pedagogies opportunities for deep, connected learning can be found. Treat students as partners and change agents and they will find deep learning.
> - Look outside to learn - work with others in different teams, disciplines, situations and community locations. You will find new ideas.
> - Think big - education is 'in the forefront of figuring out the future of humankind' (Fullan and Hargreaves, 2016: 22). Get involved with others in 'part of this life-changing and world-changing movement' (2016: 22).

What does it mean to be a people-centred teacher?

Before the concluding message of the book, I have drawn together in one place a reminder of what it means to be a people-centred teacher.

The people-centred vision of education

The concept of 'people-centred teaching' represents a vision of education as an ongoing process drawing individuals, groups and communities together to support them in determining and achieving their own goals, destiny and purpose. This springs from a belief that individuals and groups are naturally as humans able to learn, work and live together and that education can provide opportunities to help that process to work at all levels.

Acts of connection

The creation of 'connections to the past and future' through deep, engaged learning should be one of the most significant goals of a people-centred teacher and a powerful vehicle for the construction and sharing of those experiences is the use of 'acts of connection'.

The connected professional

As a 'connected professional' you will be able to help students make those connections which can lead to learning, and make connections with other teaching professionals and the community at large. You will create and use acts of connection to help your students learn in a people-centred way.

The model of the connected professional contains four 'connections', which are:

1 The Practical Connection – the practical teaching skills, knowledge, understanding and application which are essential for all teachers to be able to carry out their role.

2 The Democratic Connection – the active involvement in action where practitioners work together democratically with other colleagues towards agreed goals.

3   The Civic Connection – active participation in civic action with the wider community to support development with and for that community.

4   The Network Connection – seeking, undertaking and sustaining active engagement with other professionals and the wider community.

Characteristics addressed by people-centred teaching

People-centred teaching and learning works with the student as a whole person, but there are some human characteristics which are particularly important and they are empathy and trust; self-concept; motivation and aspiration; creativity and communication.

Professional values

The professional values of people-centred teachers in FE should be to:

- Conduct their profession with honesty, integrity and transparency within the public domain.

- Accept responsibility for a social purpose within their specialism and a broader purpose in the wider community beyond that.

- Accept the responsibility to work with other professionals and the wider community.

- Support students through their commitment, humanity, organisation and professional expertise.

- Find ways of improving teaching and learning.

- Care for each other as a fundamental prerequisite for mental and emotional well- being.

- Demonstrate autonomy within their professional practice.

- Participate in decisions affecting their professional lives and environments.

- Subject their work to public accountability.

- Selflessly commit to updating their expertise and continuous development of their field.

Building trust

People-centred teachers use strategies such as 'helping skills' and 'student-centred learning' for building trust between teachers and students, between and among students, and between teachers and other teachers. You will make use of the good evidence about how these strategies and teaching interventions do help to build student confidence, motivation, creativity and achievement.

You will seek collaboration with other teachers and make use of democratic approaches such as relational leadership to help that collaboration and teamwork to build inter-professional trust.

You will appreciate and celebrate the value of golden moments in teaching and learning, and understand how to positively manage troubled times.

Being organised

Being people-centred as a teacher is essential, but being people-centred is less likely to succeed if you are not also organised. Being organised involves:

- matters of the head – developing the self-awareness and self-confidence needed to be a teacher

- matters of the heart – taking account of supporting emotional engagement and emotional well-being for teachers and students

- managing your teaching – carrying out curriculum and session planning using approaches such as 'constructive alignment' and ASSUREd planning

- helping your students manage themselves – applying approaches such as Tuckman's to group dynamics to help build trust between your students

- managing your own career – claiming and enacting the positive autonomous characteristics of an FE teaching professional.

Characteristics of an FE teaching professional

Gregson at al.'s (2015) vision of the characteristics of an FE teaching professional include being able to:

- achieve 'satisfaction, commitment, well-being and effectiveness' (2015: 14)

- achieve a 'healthy balance between personal, work and external policy challenges' (2015: 14)

- draw 'coherence from their underlying values and beliefs' (2015: 14)

- have a capacity to affect their learners in 'positive, educational and life-enhancing ways' (2015: 14).

Being connected by digital technology

The metaphor of the 'digital swamp' highlights some of the challenges, issues and mistakes that education has already made, and continues to make when using digital technologies. People-centred teachers use their understanding from the best available evidence of what can and does work when using digital technologies to support their students' learning.

You will make use of network learning and this will include reaching out to and engaging with the wider community, and you will strive to 'make technology human'.

Global citizenship, critical thinking and a local community focus

Remaining aware of the global education challenges and relating that to inequality in your own country are important in the people-centred teacher's goal to improve social mobility.

You will utilise critical reflection, 'reflection-in-action' and 'reflection-on-action' to assist with the 'mix and match' of your teaching choices and extend and act on this critical thinking through practitioner research. Practitioner research will help you and others to stand together and stand out, and develop new practices and principles of teaching.

You will seek opportunities to broaden the civic connections in your working life so that the transformative benefits of people-centred teaching in FE can extend to all.

A people-centred teacher is a people-centred person.

Spotlight on pedagogy and reflective learning exercise

A final act of connection – education, education, education

One of the most important recent publications about further education, its problems and how they could be solved was written by Frank Coffield, and published back in 2008. *Just suppose teaching and learning became the first priority* . . . is a powerful, coherent and authoritative critique of FE from one of its best advocates. Coffield forcefully ridicules some of the managerialist and oppressive over emphasis on education for primarily economic benefits in FE, and also makes recommendations which are well worth repeating here:

We need a new set of priorities for the sector and I wish to suggest the following:

- to inspire and enable individuals to develop their capacities to the highest potential levels throughout life, so that they grow intellectually, are well equipped for work, can contribute effectively to society and achieve personal fulfilment

- to serve the needs of an adaptable, sustainable knowledge-based economy [and society] at local, regional and national levels

- to play a major role in shaping a democratic, civilised, inclusive society

- to increase knowledge and understanding for their own sake and to foster their application to the benefit of the economy and society.

(Coffield, 2008: 59–60)

Take a look at these four recommendations from Coffield, and ask yourself these very big questions:

- Can I and do I inspire and enable individuals to develop their capacities to the highest potential levels throughout life?

- How does my teaching work contribute to serving the needs of an adaptable, sustainable knowledge-based economy [and society] at local, regional and national levels?

- What role do I play in shaping a democratic, civilised, inclusive society?

- How have I increased knowledge and understanding for their own sake and fostered their application to the benefit of the economy and society?

This chapter

This chapter firstly introduced resilience as a quality needed by teachers and their students and considered how a 'growth mindset' can help to develop it. Practical advice about managing the 'three Ps of pressure' and suggestions about preparing for inspection by 'getting inside' Ofsted then followed. A consideration of how to promote 'learning careers' with your students and how teachers can achieve lengthy 'teaching careers' was provided and the chapter then moved to its conclusion with a reminder of the key ideas, principles and practice of people-centred teaching.

Just suppose we can just teach

As you move towards becoming connected professionals who just teach with people-centred teaching, let Frank Coffield's closing words from 'Just suppose' warm your hearts.

> Moreover, something vital to the whole enterprise is being forgotten. I learned from my father, as he learned from his, to hear the music, the excitement and the hope in the word 'education'. I also learned that it is the job of teachers to help other people's children to hear and respond to that music. We do it because teaching is a noble profession, which dedicates itself to the lot of those who have not had our advantages. We do it because we believe in social justice and, like our parents and grandparents, we want a better world for ourselves, our children and all children. That is the meaning of our lives as teachers.

Notes for further reading

Bloomer, M. and Hodkinson, P. (2000) Learning careers: continuity and change in young people's dispositions to learning. *British Educational Research Journal*, 26(5), pp. 583-597.

This research was in my view one of the most important FE-based works undertaken at its time, and it is still relevant now, so is well worth a read. If you can't access the shorter journal article, search for "Bloomer and Hodkinson" in Google Scholar, and you will find the longer report about the research.

Coffield, F. (2008) *Just suppose teaching and learning became the first priority*. . . London: Learning and Skills Network.

It may be nearly ten years old, but do take the time to download it (easily available online). I challenge you not to cheer at least once as you read what Frank has to say, and how he manages to say it.

Fullan, M. and Hargreaves, A. (2016) Bringing the profession back in: Call to action. Oxford, OH: Learning Forward

You shouldn't have any trouble locating this publication online. Two big current names in world education combine in this publication to produce some very interesting thinking on 'good old pedagogies', 'good new pedagogies' and more besides. It makes interesting reading but also has some very important recommendations.

National standards which are addressed by this chapter are:

1. Reflect on what works best in your teaching and learning to meet the diverse needs of learners.

2. Evaluate and challenge your practice, values and beliefs.

3. Inspire, motivate and raise aspirations of learners through your enthusiasm and knowledge.

4. Be creative and innovative in selecting and adapting strategies to help learners to learn.

5. Value and promote social and cultural diversity, equality of opportunity and inclusion.

6. Build positive and collaborative relationships with colleagues and learners.

7. Maintain and update knowledge of your subject and/or vocational area.

8. Maintain and update your knowledge of educational research to develop evidence-based practice.

9. Apply theoretical understanding of effective practice in teaching, learning and assessment drawing on research and other evidence.

10. Evaluate your practice with others and assess its impact on learning.

11. Manage and promote positive learner behaviour.

12. Understand the teaching and professional role and your responsibilities.

13. Motivate and inspire learners to promote achievement and develop their skills to enable progression.

15. Promote the benefits of technology and support learners in its use.

17. Enable learners to share responsibility for their own learning and assessment, setting goals that stretch and challenge.

19. Maintain and update your teaching and training expertise and vocational skills through collaboration with employers.

20. Contribute to organisational development and quality improvement through collaboration with others.

References

Adams, D. (1979) The Hitchhiker's Guide to the Galaxy. London: Pan.

Anna Freud Research Centre and Public Health England (2016) Measuring and Monitoring Children and Young People's Mental Wellbeing: A Toolkit for Schools and Colleges. London: Public Health England.

ACETT (2015) *TEST Project Final Report*. Taunton: Association of Centres for Excellence in Teacher Training.

AoC (2015) *College Key Facts 2014–2015*. London: Association of Colleges.

Aubrey, K. and Riley, A. (2015) *Understanding and Using Educational Theories*. London: SAGE.

Avis, J., Bathmaker, A.M. and Parsons, J. (2002) Communities of practice and the construction of learners in post-compulsory education and training. *Journal of Vocational Education and Training*, 54(1), pp.27–50.

Barchard, K.A. (2003) Does emotional intelligence assist in the prediction of academic success? Educational and Psychological Measurement, 63, pp. 840-858.

Biesta, G. (2010) *Good Education in an Age of Measurement: Ethics, Politics, Democracy*. Colorado: Paradigm Pubs.

Biggs, J. (2003) *Aligning Teaching for Constructing Learning*. York: Higher Education Academy.

Bloomer, M. and Hodkinson, P. (2000) Learning careers: continuity and change in young people's dispositions to learning. *British Educational Research Journal*, 26(5), pp. 583–597.

Bonebright, D.A. (2010) 40 years of storming: A historical review of Tuckman's model of small group development. *Human Resource Development International*, 13(1), pp.111–120.

Brandes, D. and Ginnis, P. (1996) *A Guide to Student-centred Learning*. Leicester: Nelson Thornes.

Buckingham, D. and Jones, K. (2001) New Labour's cultural turn: some tensions in contemporary educational and cultural policy. *Journal of Education Policy*, 16(1), pp. 1–14.

Butler Act (1944) *The Cabinet Papers 1915–1982*. London: HMSO.

Clow, A. and Palmer, S. (2004) *The Stress Test*. London: British Broadcasting Corporation.

Coffield, F. (2008) *Just Suppose Teaching and Learning Became the First Priority* . . . London: Learning and Skills Network.

Coffield, F. (2017) *Will the Leopard Change its Spots? A New Model of Inspection for Ofsted*. London: IoE UCL press.

Crawley, J. (2010) *In at the Deep End. A Survival Guide for Teachers in Post-compulsory Education.* 2nd ed. London: Routledge.

Crawley, J. (2015) Growing connections – the connected professional. *Research in Post-Compulsory Education,* 20(4), pp. 476–498.

Department for Business, Innovation and Skills (2012) *Professionalism in Further Education, Interim Report.* London: DBIS.

Department for Education (2017) *The Technical and Further Education Act (2017).* London: HMSO.

Dewey, J. (1916). *Democracy and Education: An Introduction to the Philosophy of Education.* New York: Macmillan.

Domitrovich C.E., Bradshaw C.P., Greenberg M.T., Embry D., Poduska J.M., and Ialongo N.S. (2010) Integrated models of school-based prevention: Logic and theory. *Psychology in the Schools,* (47), pp.71–88. doi: 10.1002/pits.20452

Duckworth, V. (2016) Enacting teacher education values. In: Crawley, J. (ed.), *Post Compulsory Teacher Educators. Connecting Professionals,* 1st ed. Northwich: Critical Publishing, pp.34–41.

Duckworth, V. and Smith, R. (2017) *Further Education in England: Transforming Lives and Communities – Interim report.* London: Universities and Colleges Union.

Dweck, C.S. (2006) *Mindset: The New Psychology of Success.* New York: Random House.

Dzur, A.W. (2008). *Democratic Professionalism: Citizen Participation and the Reconstruction of Professional Ethics, Identity, and Practice.* Pennsylvania: Penn State Press.

Education and Training Foundation (2014) *Professional Standards for Teachers and Trainers – England.* London: Education and Training Foundation.

Education Endowment Foundation (2017) *'Evaluation FAQs'.* [online] at https://educationendowment foundation.org.uk/our-work/the-eefs-approach-to-evaluation/faqs/ Accessed 02/08/17.

Education Endowment Foundation (2017a) *'Teaching and Learning Toolkit'.* [online] at https://education endowmentfoundation.org.uk/resources/teaching-learning-toolkit/ Accessed 02/08/17.

Education Endowment Foundation (2017b) *Evidence Summary: Collaborative Learning.* London: EEF.

Education Endowment Foundation (2017c) *Evidence Summary: Peer Tutoring.* London: EEF.

Education Endowment Foundation (2017d) *Evidence Summary: Social and Emotional Learning.* London: EEF.

Education and Training Foundation (2017e) *Outstanding Teaching, Learning and Assessment.* [online] http://www.et-foundation.co.uk/supporting/support-practitioners/improvements-in-teacher-learning-and-assessment/ Accessed 16/07/17.

Egan, G. (1994) *The Skilled Helper.* California: Brooks/Cole Pubs.

Elkjaer, B. (2010) Pragmatism: A Learning Theory for the Future. In: Illeris, K. (2010). (ed.) *Contemporary Theories of Learning.* London: Routledge. pp. 74–89.

Engestrom, Y. (2010) Expansive learning: toward an activity theoretical reconceptualization. In: Illeris, K. (ed.) *Contemporary Theories of Learning.* Abingdon: Routledge, pp.53–73.

Fenwick, T. and Tennant, M. (2004). Understanding Adult Learners in Foley, G. (Ed). *Dimensions of Adult Learning: Adult Education and Training in a Global Era*. Sydney: Allen & Unwin. pp 55–73.

Fisher, R. and Simmons, R. (2010) *What is the lifelong learning sector?* In: Avis, J., Fisher, R. and Thompson, R. (eds), *Teaching in Lifelong Learning. A Guide to Theory and Practice*. 1st ed. Maidenhead: Open University Press, pp.8–17.

Freedman, D.M., Bullock, P.L. and Duque, G.S. (2005) Teacher educators' reflections on moments in a secondary teacher education course: Thinking forward by challenging our teaching practices. *Teachers and Teaching: Theory and Practice*. 11(6), pp. 591–602.

Freire, P. (1973) *Pedagogy of the Oppressed*. 11th ed. New York: Herder and Herder.

Fullan, M. and Donnelly, K. (2015) *Evaluating and Assessing Tools in the Digital Swamp*. Bloomington, IN: Solution Tree Press.

Fullan, M. and Hargreaves, A. (2016) *Bringing the Profession Back In: Call to Action*. Oxford, OH: Learning Forward.

Fuller, A. and Unwin, L. (2003). Learning as apprentices in the contemporary UK workplace: Creating and managing expansive and restrictive participation. *Journal of Education and Work*, 16(4), pp.407–426.

Gagne, R. (1985) *The Conditions of Learning*, 4th.ed. New York: Holt, Rinehart & Winston.

General Teaching Council (2008) *Research for Teachers. Carl Rogers and the Classroom Climate*. London: GTC.

Gregson, M., Hillier, Y., Biesta, G., Duncan, S., Nixon, L., Spedding, T. and Wakeling, P. (2015) *Reflective Teaching in Further, Adult and Vocational Education*. Bloomsbury Publishing.

Grigar, D. (2013) hooks in the 21st Century: Feminist Pedagogy in Action. Conference contribution to Digital Humanities 2013 conference. [online] http://dtc-wsuv.org/wp/dh2013/ Accessed 27/07/17.

Gutman, L. and Akerman, R. (2008) *Determinants of Aspirations [wider benefits of learning research report no. 27]*. Centre for Research on the Wider Benefits of Learning. London: Institute of Education, University of London.

Hafez, R. (2015) *Beyond the metaphor: Time to Take Over the Castle*. In Daley, M., Orr, K., Petrie, J., (Eds.) *Further Education and the 12 Dancing Princesses*. London. IOE/Trentham, Pp. 157–164.

Haley, Shelly (1995). Practicing freedom. *The Women's Review of Books*, 7(6), pp. 10–11.

Hargreaves, A. (2003) *Teaching in the Knowledge Society: Education in the Age of Insecurity*. London: Teachers College Press.

Hattie, J. (2012) *Visible Learning for Teachers: Maximizing Impact on Learning*. London: Routledge.

Higgins, S., Xiao, Z. and Katsipataki, M. (2012) *The Impact of Digital Technology on Learning: A Summary for the Education Endowment Foundation*. Durham, UK: Education Endowment Foundation and Durham University.

Hillier, Y. (2002) *Reflective Teaching in Further and Adult Education*. London: Continuum.

hooks, bell (2003) *Teaching Community. A Pedagogy of Hope*. New York: Routledge.

hooks, bell (1994) *Teaching to Transgress. Education as the Practice of Freedom*. London: Routledge.

Hopson, B. and Scally, M. (1999). *Build your own Rainbow: a Workbook for Career and Life Management*. 3rd ed. Chalford: Management books.

Hopson, B. and Scally, M (2013) *The Ultimate Life Skill: Live Happier*. Leeds: Livehappier Ltd.

Huberman, M. (1989) The professional life cycle of teachers. *Teachers College Record*, 91(1), pp.31–57.

Illeris, K. (2010). Ed. *Contemporary Theories of Learning*. London: Routledge.

Independent Commission on Colleges in their Communities (UK) (2011) *A Dynamic Nucleus: Colleges at the Heart of Local Communities*: The Final Report of the Independent Commission on Colleges in their Communities. Leicester: NIACE.

Jarvis, P. (2010) Learning to be a person in society: Learning to be me. In: Illeris, K. (Ed.) *Contemporary Theories of Learning*. London: Routledge. pp. 21–34.

Lachapelle, P. (2011). The use of social networking in community development. *CD Practice*, 17, pp.1–8.

Lacom, C. and Hadley, S. (2009) *Teaching to Transgress: Deconstructing Normalcy and Resignifiying the Marked Body*. In del Guadalupe Davidson, M. and Yancy, G. (Eds.), *Critical perspectives on bell hooks*. New York: Routledge, pp 55–67.

Langford R., Bonell C., Jones H., Pouliou T., Murphy S. and Waters E. (2014) The WHO Health Promoting School framework for Improving the Health and Well-being of Students and their Academic Achievement. *Cochrane Database Syst Rev* (4) doi: 10.1002/14651858.CD008958.pub2

Laurillard, D. (2012) *Teaching as a Design Science: Building Pedagogical Patterns for Learning and Technology*. New York City: Routledge.

Lave, J. and Wenger, E. (1991) *Situated Learning: Legitimate Peripheral Participation*. Cambridge: Cambridge University Press.

Luckin, R., Bligh, B., Manches, A., Ainsworth, S., Crook, C. and Noss, R. (2012) *Decoding Learning: The Proof, Promise and Potential of Digital Education*. London: NESTA.

Lunenberg, M., Korthagen, F. and Swennen, A. (2007) The teacher educator as role model. *Teaching and Teacher Education*, 23(5), pp. 586–601.

Margolin, J., Haynes, E., Heppen, J., Ruedel, K., Meakin, J., Hauser, A. and Hubbard, A. (2014) *Evaluation of the Common Core Technology Project*. Washington: American Institutes for Research.

Maslow, Abraham H. (1954) *Personality and Motivation*. Harlow: Longman.

Matthews, G., Roberts, R.D. and Zeidner, M. (2004). Seven myths about emotional intelligence. *Psychological Inquiry*, 15, pp. 179–196.

McQueen, H.A., Shields, C., Finnegan, D.J., Higham, J. and Simmen, M.W. (2014) Peerwise provides significant academic benefits to biological science students across diverse learning tasks, but with minimal instructor intervention. *Biochemistry and Molecular Biology Education*, 42(5), pp.371–381.

Munday, I. (2014) Creativity: performativity's poison or its antidote? *Cambridge Journal of Education*, 44(3), pp. 319–332.

Nesbit, T., Leach, L. and Foley, G. (2004) Teaching adults. In Foley, G. (Ed.) *Dimensions of Learning: Adult Education and Training in a Global Era*. Maidenhead: Open University Press.

OECD (2017a) *About PISA* [online] http://www.oecd.org/pisa/aboutpisa/ Accessed 18/07/17.

Ofsted (2017b) *About us* [online] https://www.gov.uk/government/organisations/ofsted/about Accessed 03/08/17.

Ofsted (2017c) *Further Education and Skills Inspection Handbook.* London: Office for Standards in Education.

Orr, K. (2016) The filling in the educational sandwich: Post compulsory education. In: Crawley, J. (Ed.) *Post Compulsory Teacher Educators. Connecting Professionals,* 1st ed. Northwich: Critical Publishing, pp.16–23.

Pearson, E.M. (1999) Humanism and individualism: Maslow and his critics. *Adult Education Quarterly,* 50, pp. 41–55.

Pettis, Joyce (1986) A review of feminist theory: From Margin To Center. *Journal of Women in Culture and Society.* 11 (4), pp. 788–789.

Petty, G. (2006) *Evidence-Based Teaching – A Practical Approach.* Cheltenham: Nelson Thornes.

Pleasance, S. (2016) *Wider Professional Practice in Education and Training.* London: SAGE.

Race, P. (2014) *Making Learning Happen. A Guide for Post-Compulsory Education.* 3rd ed. London: SAGE.

Reaburn, P., Muldoon, N. and Bookallil, C. (2009) *Blended Spaces, Work Based Learning and Constructive Alignment: Impacts on Student Engagement.* In Proceedings of ASCILITE – Australian Society for Computers in Learning in Tertiary Education Annual Conference 2009 (pp. 820–831). Australasian Society for Computers in Learning in Tertiary Education. [online] https://www.learntechlib.org/p/46431/ Accessed 21/7/17.

Reale, P. (2009) Glimpsing the whole at a glance: Using pictures and images to help teacher trainees make sense of the action research journey. In Appleby, Y. and Banks, C. (Eds.) *Looking Back and Moving Forward. Reflecting on our Practice as Teacher Educators.* Preston: University of Central Lancashire, pp 27–38.

Roberts, J. (2006) Limits to communities of practice. *Journal of Management Studies,* 43(3), pp. 623–639.

Robinson, K. (2001) All Our Futures: Creativity, Culture and Education. Sudbury: DfEE.

Robinson, K. (2011) *Out of our Minds. Learning to be Creative.* Chichester: Capstone Publishing.

Rogers, C. R. (1961) *On Becoming a Person: A Therapist's View of Psychology.* London: Constable.

Rogers, C. R. (1990) *The Carl Rogers Reader.* Eds. Kirschenbaum, H. and Land Henderson, V. London: Constable.

Sachs, J. (2000) The activist professional. *Journal of Educational Change,* 1(1), pp. 77–94.

Schon, D. (1983) *The Reflective Practitioner. How Professionals Think in Action.* London: Temple Smith.

Sebba, J., Kent, P. and Tregenza, J. (2010) *Joint Practice Development: What does the Evidence Suggest are Effective Approaches.* National College for School Leadership: Nottingham.

Smith, M. K. (2004) *Carl Rogers and Informal Education, the Encyclopaedia of Informal Education.* [online] www.infed.org/thinkers/et-rogers.htm. [online] Accessed 03/07/2017.

Social Mobility Commission (2017) Time for Change: An Assessment of Government Policies on Social Mobility 1997–2017. London: Social Mobility Commission.

Stephens, J.P. and Carmeli, A. (2015) Relational leadership and creativity: The effects of respectful engagement and caring on meaningfulness and creative work involvement. In. Hemlin, S. and Mumford, M. D. (Eds.) *Handbook of Research on Creativity and Leadership*. Cheltenham: Edward Elgar.

Stewart-Brown, S. (2000) Parenting, well-being, health and disease. In Buchanan, A. and Hudson, B. (Eds.) *Promoting Children's Emotional Well-being*. Oxford: Oxford University Press, pp. 28–47.

Sutter, J. and McCluskey, L. (2016) *OTLA Case Study: Clean Break*. London: Education and Training Foundation.

Tarling, J. (2016) Could flow psychology change the way we think about vocational learning and stem the tide of poor wellbeing affecting our students? Ask the students, they'll tell you. *Research in Post-Compulsory Education*, 21(3), pp.302–305.

Team Raddicati (2015) *Email Statistics Report, 2015–2019*. California: The Radicati Group.

UNESCO (2017) *Education Transforms Lives*. Paris: United Nations Educational, Scientific and Cultural Organization.

Veugelers, W. and O'Hair, M.J. (2005). *Network Learning for Educational Change*. Maidenhead: Open University Press.

Villeneuve-Smith, F., Munoz, S. and McKenzie, E. (2008) *FE Colleges: The Frontline Under Pressure*. London: Learning and Skills Network (LSN).

Wadkins, T., Wozniak, W. and Miller, R.L. (2004) Team teaching models. In. *UNK/CTE, Compendium of Teaching Resources and Ideas*. New England: University of Nebraska, pp.77–95.

Walker, M. (2012) The Origins and Development of the Mechanics' Institute Movement 1824 – 1890 and the Beginnings of Further Education. *Teaching in Lifelong Learning: A Journal to Inform and Improve Practice*, 4(1), pp. 32–39.

Wallace, S. (2014) When you're smiling: Exploring how teachers motivate and engage learners in the further education sector. *Journal of Further and Higher Education*, 38(3), pp.346–360.

Wang, X., Su, Y., Cheung, S., Wong, E. and Kwong, T. (2013) An exploration of Biggs' constructive alignment in course design and its impact on students' learning approaches. *Assessment & Evaluation in Higher Education*, 38(4), pp.477–491.

Warwick, I., Maxwell, C., Simon, A., Statham, J. and Aggleton, P. (2006) *Mental Health and Emotional Well-being of Students in Further Education - A Scoping Study*. London: Thomas Coram Research Unit Institute of Education.

Weare, K. (2004) *Developing the Emotionally Literate School*. London: SAGE.

Wenger, E. (2010) A social theory of learning. In: Illeris, K. (Ed.) *Contemporary Theories of Learning*. London: Routledge. pp. 209–218.

Wood, I. (2015) *Why we Need a Global Human/Technology Manifesto*. Campaign. [online] http://www.campaignlive.co.uk/article/why-need-global-human-technology-manifesto/1341666 Accessed 17/07/2017.

Index